Refresh
Your Soul

Refresh
Your Soul

60 Devotions
to Help You
Rest in the Lord

WORTHY®
Inspired

Compiled by Jill Jones
Cover design by Jeff Jansen | AestheticSoup.com
Cover art by Shutterstock
Interior design by Bart Dawson

Printed in the United States of America

2 3 4 5 6 7 8 9 LBM 21 20 19 18 17

I will refresh the weary
and satisfy the faint.

JEREMIAH 31:25 NIV

Introduction

It's okay to take a moment. To stop. Disconnect. Close your eyes. Pray. When time and options are running low, when anxiety, fear, or worry are crowding in and stealing your breath, God is just a prayer away.

Refresh your soul with these sixty short devotions. Let them help you connect to Jesus and give you peace of mind that only He can give. Let Him touch your heart as only He can.

Carve out five minutes a day to absorb the wisdom and insight from these fresh messages and you will feel restored and ready for what the day may bring. Just breathe. God has this day.

Day 1

Time for a Beauty Break

How many are your works, LORD! In wisdom
you made them all; the earth is full of your creatures.

PSALM 104:24 NIV

We hurry, worry, and try to somehow hold it all together. The chaos of modern life leaves us dazed, and daily stress can shrivel our souls.

A simple remedy exists with the power to refresh us at our core. We can take a beauty break—a pause to relish God and marvel at His creation.

Beauty hints of another world, the world of order and peace where God, our intelligent designer, dwells. Beauty awakens our hearts to worship and connects us to the One who makes all things beautiful in His time.

Step outside for fifteen minutes to drink in creation's glory. You might see a butterfly take flight or let the sunset steal your breath away. You might stoop down to admire a pansy or watch a squirrel scamper up a tree. Sidestep your desk or that sink full of dishes to exhale and remember how our Father plants beauty everywhere.

Psalm 104 revels in creation's beauty and reminds us to praise its Maker. It concludes with these words in verse 33: "I will sing to the LORD all my life; I will sing praise to my God as long as I live" (NIV).

Short beauty breaks train our minds to behold and bask in God's presence. Let beauty become the maestro of your heart, leading you to nonstop adoration of the Creator.

Father, teach me to pause throughout the day to glimpse Your beauty. Refresh my soul as I behold Your handiwork. Thank You for Your incredible creation. Amen.

I love to think of nature as an unlimited broadcasting station, through which God speaks to us every hour, if we will only tune in.

GEORGE WASHINGTON CARVER

All that is good, all that is true, all that is beautiful, all that is beneficent, be it great or small, be it perfect or fragmentary, natural as well as supernatural, moral as well as material, comes from God.

JOHN HENRY NEWMAN

May the glory of the LORD continue forever!
The LORD takes pleasure
in all he has made!...
I will sing to the LORD as long as I live.
I will praise my God to my last breath!...
Let all that I am praise the LORD.

PSALM 104:31, 33, 35 NLT

Day 2

New Every Morning

His compassions never fail.
They are new every morning; great is your faithfulness.
LAMENTATIONS 3:22–23 NIV

I'm partial to late spring daybreaks. I experience them through a filter, as the encroaching rays tickle my eyelids. (I'm never sure—do I see through the membranes, or is there a not-quite-closed gap?) Contours begin to materialize, and the chirrups of birds provide a captivating backdrop.

"As each day comes to us refreshed and anew," enthuses Terri Guillemets, "so does my gratitude renew itself daily. The breaking of the sun over the horizon is my grateful heart dawning upon a blessed world." It's wonderful to awake in gratitude, yes, but the dawn has nothing to do with my heart. In a more apt metaphor, the reemergence of the morning sun is God's gracious heart revitalizing His creation. Thankfulness is my appropriate response.

I chuckle to recall my granddaughter, pleased with some trifle, observing solemnly from her car seat behind me, "This is a great day for me." I have great days too; typically, they're mundane—the kind of day that starts out uneventfully but ends up being fulfilling and complete, the kind of day that precedes the kind of evening when my lips utter "thank You, God, for a *good* day" as my head hits the pillow.

Teach me, faithful God, to bracket my days with praise.
Thank You for fresh new mercies every morning. Amen.

Return to your rest, O my soul, for the LORD has dealt bountifully with you.

PSALM 116:7 NKJV

I will give thanks to the LORD with my whole heart; I will recount all of your wonderful deeds.

PSALM 9:1 ESV

If there was ever a secret for unleashing God's powerful peace in a situation, it's developing a heart of true thanksgiving.

LYSA TERKEURST

A sensible thanksgiving
for mercies received is a mighty prayer
in the Spirit of God.
It prevails with Him unspeakably.

JOHN BUNYAN

Day 3

A Week of Primitive Living

Then, because so many people were coming
and going that they did not even have a chance to eat,
he said to them, "Come with me by yourselves
to a quiet place and get some rest."

MARK 6:31 NIV

While my son looked forward to summer camp, I anticipated a week at a friend's cabin. After an exhausting year, the prospect of spending time with two sisters in Christ promised the perfect respite. I could hardly wait.

"Just as a heads up," my friend Anne warned me, "Rebecca's cabin doesn't have internet access or cell service. There's a landline for urgent calls."

For once, I didn't mind! Normally, I would take my laptop to work on a writing project. This time I left it at home. If I wrote, it would be in my journal with a pen. I expected to go through withdrawal. I didn't. Instead of spending the week fighting the pull of a screen, my friends and I took walks, sat on the deck, and enjoyed long talks and fits of laughter. We turned on the TV only to watch old movies at night. I went home rejuvenated.

Jesus knew when His disciples needed rest, and He knows when our best refreshment will come from trading technology for time with people and enjoying His creation.

Lord, provide a place to rest when my soul is tired. Amen.

Rest time is not waste time. It is economy to gather fresh strength…. It is wisdom to take occasional furlough. In the long run, we shall do more by sometimes doing less.

CHARLES SPURGEON

My beloved speaks and says to me: "Arise, my love, my beautiful one, and come away."

SONG OF SOLOMON 2:10 ESV

[God] cannot be found in noise and restlessness. God is the friend of silence. See how nature—trees, flowers, grass—grows in silence; see the stars, the moon, and the sun, how they move in silence…. We need silence to be able to touch souls.

MOTHER TERESA

As a child of God, how much more
do we need times of complete solitude—
times to deal with the spiritual realities
of life and to be alone with God the Father.
If there was ever anyone who could
dispense with special times of solitude
and fellowship, it was our Lord.
Yet even He could not maintain
His full strength and power for His work
and His fellowship with the Father
without His quiet time.

LETTIE B. COWMAN

Day 4

The Source of All My Joy

Send out your light and your truth; let them guide me.
Let them lead me to your holy mountain, to the place
where you live. There I will go to the altar of God,
to God—the source of all my joy.

PSALM 43:3–4 NLT

Do you ever think about God as joyful? Too often, I think
of God as a strict taskmaster who demands hard work and
perfection. However, Psalm 43 reminds me that God is the
"source of all my joy."

That means that God doesn't just dole out joy if there
is some left over; He invented it. In fact, He's the only One
in the universe who truly experiences joy in its fullness,
because His joy is not tainted by sin. Therefore, if I want
joy, the only place I'm going to find it is from its source.

Right before proclaiming God as the source of all joy,
the psalmist writes about God's light and truth that guide
us to His "holy mountain" where God lives, which is an
invitation to be with Him. We get to hang out with God!
Just thinking about that gives me incredible joy.

Lord, help me not to look for joy in all the wrong places;
instead, help me to understand that You
are the most joyful Being in the universe. Amen.

The joy of the LORD is your strength.

NEHEMIAH 8:10 ESV

It is His joy that remains in us that makes our joy full.

A. B. SIMPSON

Though you have not seen him, you love him; and even though you do not see him now, you believe in him and are filled with an inexpressible and glorious joy.

1 PETER 1:8 NIV

His anger is but for a moment, His favor is for a lifetime; weeping may last for the night, but a shout of joy comes in the morning.

PSALM 30:5 NASB

Seek to cultivate a buoyant,
joyous sense of the crowded kindnesses
of God in your daily life.

ALEXANDER MACLAREN

Day 5

·····❧❦❧·····

Time for Pie

A friend loves at all times,
and a brother is born for a time of adversity.
<small>PROVERBS 17:17 NIV</small>

I've never been one to seek comfort in food, so it felt out of character for me when a friend and I started a routine of declaring it "time for pie" when one or both of us were having a rough week. Was it wrong to hop in the car and head to Nation's for coconut cream or chocolate or blueberry cheesecake when we needed a break from whatever happened to be driving us crazy, instead of running to God? Then I realized that, for us, it wasn't about the pie.

We weren't seeking comfort in the cream, chocolate, sugar, or free coffee refills. We were craving that connection that made life doable again. God had placed us in each other's lives at a time when we both needed support. Whenever He provided time for pie, it felt like His way of answering the true cry of my heart or my friend's—a need for a hug, for encouragement, to be heard, to escape the ordinary.

God knows when we need Him alone and when we need to be refreshed by a friend's presence. Something about those special moments makes trusting Him a little easier.

Thank You, Lord, for the gift of friends
who revive my spirit. Amen.

We are comforted. And besides our own comfort, we rejoiced still more at the joy of Titus, because his spirit has been refreshed by you all.

2 CORINTHIANS 7:13 ESV

As iron sharpens iron, so a friend sharpens a friend.

PROVERBS 27:17 NLT

Friendship is born at that moment when one person says to another: "What! You too? I thought I was the only one."

C. S. LEWIS

One who has unreliable friends soon comes to ruin, but there is a friend who sticks closer than a brother.

PROVERBS 18:24 NIV

He is your friend
who pushes you nearer to God.

Abraham Kuyper

Day 6

Motion Wellness

*The angel of the LORD came again a second time
and touched him and said, "Arise, eat,
because the journey is too great for you."*

1 KINGS 19:7 NASB

I've experienced the defeat of victory enough times in my life to have developed a formula for recovery. Following an angel's plan has brought me to a refreshed, ready place to be affirmed by the still, small voice of God.

Elijah brought the people to a decision at the showdown on Mount Carmel. He prepared a sacrifice, rebuilt the altar of challenge, and poured out twelve buckets of water. Then, though tired and spent, he triumphantly declared victory according to the Lord's word.

The victory had stretched him to his limit, however, and Elijah soon held a pity party. Threats from an evil queen added to his exhaustion. A ministering angel came to his aid, providing nourishing refreshment till he returned to battle-ready status. Yet his response lacked zeal and obedience. He had to be admonished twice to get up, eat, and go.

Like Elijah, I've been called to ministry even when I needed comfort from battle fatigue. I've learned to rest and take nourishment, then get up and move. After one call of His voice, I'm on the go, ready, refreshed, and prepared for the next journey.

Lord, Your presence refreshes me.
I depend on Your strength to get up and go.
Thank You for Your constant supply. Amen.

When I lose my perspective on life because I'm running on empty, I can soon lose my perspective on God Himself. I need to be still and feel His loving touch and hear Him say to me, "Go to sleep, rest awhile, the journey is too great for you."

JILL BRISCOE

I will pour water on the thirsty land, and streams on the dry ground.

ISAIAH 44:3 ESV

_____

I keep my eyes always on the LORD.
With him at my right hand,
I will not be shaken. Therefore my heart
is glad and my tongue rejoices;
my body also will rest secure....
You make known to me the path of life;
you will fill me with joy in your presence,
with eternal pleasures at your right hand.

PSALM 16:8–9, 11 NIV

_____

Day 7

·····❧❧❧❧❧·····

Stop and Listen

Speak, for your servant is listening.

1 SAMUEL 3:10 NIV

If we have learned anything from the widespread use of social media, it is that everyone has something to say. Where once we were reluctant to speak with strangers, now we have conversations with nearly anyone, and concerning the most delicate subjects—politics, faith, parenting, marriage.

After a while, it seems that everyone is talking but no one is listening.

I'm often guilty of that myself. It is so much simpler to give advice than to take it, and easier to talk than to listen. It's exhausting, always feeling the need to respond, the pressure to have something to say.

How refreshing it is to converse with God. There's no expectation to have an opinion, no need to respond with a comment. All you need do is listen.

Often, that takes a bit of time and practice. Even Samuel, referenced in our verse for today, needed three tries to recognize the voice of God among many others.

Don't be afraid to "waste" part of your day in silence, allowing the voice of God to penetrate the cacophony that surrounds you. You may need to switch off the notifications on your phone to receive the one most important message that will come your way today.

Speak, Lord, for Your servant is listening. Amen.

There is not in the world a kind of life more sweet and delightful than that of a continual conversation with God.

BROTHER LAWRENCE

Here I am! I stand at the door and knock. If anyone hears my voice and opens the door, I will come in and eat with that person, and they with me.

REVELATION 3:20 NIV

God speaks to me, not through the thunder and the earthquake nor through the ocean and the stars, but through the Son of Man, and speaks in a language adapted to my imperfect sight and hearing.

WILLIAM LYON PHELPS

Having your spiritual radar up
in constant anticipation of His presence—
even in the midst of the joyful chaos
and regular rhythms of your everyday living—
is paramount in hearing God, because
sometimes the place and manner you find
Him is the least spectacular you'd expect.

PRISCILLA SHIRER

Day 8

No Record

Love is patient and kind. Love is not jealous or boastful or proud or rude. It does not demand its own way. It is not irritable, and it keeps no record of being wronged.

1 CORINTHIANS 13:4–5 NLT

While mailing documents to a client one week, I forgot some of the papers. Because of my mistake, we lost several days of progress. I told my client I'd pay for the mailing costs, but he replied, "No, we'll cover the costs—love keeps no record of wrongs."

He was quoting today's verse, which teaches us how to love genuinely—not in the counterfeit way of the world. It teaches us to forget about settling the score, to instead be lavish with grace.

True love doesn't keep track of everyday wrongs, like the papers I didn't send. Love doesn't begrudge how we acted in middle school. It doesn't dwell on words spoken during our low points, our worst moments. Love has long vision that sees beyond the biggest mistakes and lets good overshadow the bad.

When we do this, we love like our heavenly Father—the One who will "hurl all our iniquities into the depths of the sea" (Micah 7:19 NIV).

---

*Father, teach me to love in a way that refreshes the soul,
both for the forgiver and the forgiven. Amen.*

Repent, then, and turn to God, so that your sins may be wiped out, that times of refreshing may come from the Lord.

ACTS 3:19 NIV

A quarrel between friends, when made up, adds a new tie to friendship. Be who you are and be that well.

FRANCIS DE SALES

Be kind to one another, tenderhearted, forgiving one another, as God in Christ forgave you.

EPHESIANS 4:32 ESV

Forgiveness is the giving, and so the receiving, of life.

GEORGE MACDONALD

I lay down my anger, unforgiveness,
and stubborn ways that beg me to build
walls when I sense hints of rejection.
I lay all these things down with my broken
boards and ask that Your holy fire consume
them until they become weightless ashes.
And as I walk away, my soul feels safe.
Held. And truly free to finally be me.

LYSA TERKEURST

Day 9

Gold Apples

A word spoken at the right time
is like gold apples on a silver tray.
PROVERBS 25:11 HCSB

Every autumn, our church holds a clothing drive. One year, many church members wanted to volunteer and donate clothes, but no one was available to chair the event. After praying, I knew God was leading me to direct it myself. I worried, though, that my effort would somehow fall short.

When the event began, so many of the volunteers were upbeat. "Look at all the clothes!" one woman said. Another said, "The turnout is fantastic." Rather than forgetting these remarks, I drank them in—knowing God was giving me the encouragement I needed. When criticisms were raised, I took them as helpful. Scripture says, "A person's wisdom yields patience; it is to one's glory to overlook an offense" (Proverbs 19:11 NIV).

Encouraging words are like a long, deep breath—they refresh us to the core. Instead of feeding the negativity that has become commonplace today, we can follow the Bible's advice to uplift others—with a touch, a smile, or a word. God will send the right people when we need the same.

———————————————

*Father, sharpen my eyes to see the gifts—big and small—
that You've sent to encourage me. Amen.*

———————————————

The Sovereign LORD has given me a well-instructed tongue, to know the word that sustains the weary.

ISAIAH 50:4 NIV

I'll lift you and you lift me, and we'll both ascend together.

JOHN GREENLEAF WHITTIER

Encouragement is awesome. It can actually change the course of another person's day, week, or life.

CHARLES R. SWINDOLL

Let us consider one another in order to stir up love and good works.

HEBREWS 10:24 NKJV

If I can put one touch of rosy sunset
into the life of any man or woman,
I shall feel that I have worked with God.

G. K. CHESTERTON

Taking a Break

Jesus said, "Let's go off by ourselves to a quiet place
and rest awhile." He said this because there were
so many people coming and going that Jesus
and his apostles didn't even have time to eat.

MARK 6:31 NLT

While on a mission trip in the rural mountains of Peru, I noticed something extraordinary about the people. When we'd greet a stranger—standing at their doorstep or in a field of potatoes—they always took time to speak with us. Never rushing to end the conversation, they were happy to take a break and enjoy our company.

Stopping to rest was important to Jesus, too. While on long journeys with His disciples, Jesus insisted on breaks that allowed them to find nourishment and avoid the crowds for a while.

One day, Jesus grew tired and stopped at Jacob's well for a drink. There He ministered to a sinful Samaritan woman, telling her about the living water of everlasting life (John 4:14). Amazed, she returned to her town to tell others about the man she'd met.

Don't feel guilty about taking a timeout when you need it. Most likely, it will refresh you for the tasks ahead. Now and then, it will lead to unforgettable moments.

Father, help me to balance my to-do list with opportunities to be refreshed, nourished, and enjoy people. Amen.

Most of the things we need to be most fully alive never come in busyness. They grow in rest.

MARK BUCHANAN

The Spirit and the Bride say, "Come." And let the one who hears say, "Come." And let the one who is thirsty come; let the one who desires take the water of life without price.

REVELATION 22:17 ESV

Yes, my soul, find rest in God; my hope comes from him. Truly he is my rock and my salvation; he is my fortress, I will not be shaken.

PSALM 62:5–6 NIV

Lord, strengthen the weary and renovate
our hearts. Revive us when we are dying
and make new the dead, the stagnant,
the broken, and the decaying.
Purify our hearts so we can find times
of refreshing in Your presence.

HEATHER C. KING

Day 11

······❧⤟❧❧❧·······

Inhaling the Wonders
of His Grace

The grace of our Lord was poured out on me abundantly,
along with the faith and love that are in Christ Jesus.

1 TIMOTHY 1:14 NIV

Inhale the wonder of grace! Take a great big breath.

Breathe grace in ever so slowly. Let it flood your whole being, your deepest places, with its refreshment.

Grace is always there. Abundant. It never runs out. It's both a one-time download and an ongoing gift. Glorious grace means you live every single second forgiven and free. You are fully accepted every minute. Every hour you are empowered to live in God's strength, wisdom, and care.

Grace means you have 24/7 access to all that God is. His joy. His hope. His peace.

When Jesus saved you, He didn't only give you a ticket to eternal life. He flooded you with the grace you need to live this life too. His grace seals the love and faith that are natural parts of who He is, and He plants that love and faith inside of you. Living in grace means understanding that God looks upon you with delight. He doesn't condemn. He doesn't frown at you. He loves you! God is excited about who you are and who He is empowering you to become.

Thank You, Lord, for the joy of living
and breathing grace! Amen.

Grace is given not because we have done good works but in order that we may be able to do them.

ST. AUGUSTINE

God, being rich in mercy, because of His great love with which He loved us, even when we were dead in our transgressions, made us alive together with Christ (by grace you have been saved), and raised us up with Him, and seated us with Him in the heavenly places in Christ Jesus, so that in the ages to come He might show the surpassing riches of His grace in kindness toward us in Christ Jesus.

EPHESIANS 2:4–7 NASB

To be grateful is to recognize the love
of God in everything He has given us—
and He has given us everything.
Every breath we draw is a gift of His love;
every moment of existence is a grace,
for it brings with it immense
graces from Him.

THOMAS MERTON

Life Support

As a deer pants for streams of water,
so my soul pants for you, my God.
PSALM 42:1 NIV

Feeling the cool air sweeping over the ocean waves and onto the beach is a most relaxing experience. God created beaches, air, and water for enjoyment. While out basking in the summer breeze, we should take the time to pray and thank Him. He wants us to worship and adore Him.

Just as air and water support life for our bodies, so is He the life support for our souls. Without Him, we can't live the abundant life He has promised us.

Psalm 42:1 says, "As a deer pants for streams of water, so my soul pants for you, my God." A panting deer breathes hard and quickly because it has been running. Are we running after God in our daily journey?

When our son was born, our six-year-old daughter, Ellie, would get off the school bus each day and run into the house to see him. She knew he would be there waiting. She was filled with anticipation just to see him.

Shouldn't we feel this same kind of exhilaration when we talk to God? We're His children. He's waiting.

God, help me to run into Your arms today,
excited to spend time with You. Amen.

O Lord our God, grant us grace to desire Thee with our whole heart; that, so desiring, we may seek, and seeking find Thee; and so finding Thee, may love Thee.

ANSELM OF CANTERBURY

Become a man or woman of prayer.... Let your heart and mind be kept close to the principal calling of your life, which is to hunger and thirst after God and His righteousness.... Let the thoughts and intents of your heart be shaped and guided by time spent in His presence.

RAVI ZACHARIAS

Prayer is a way of language practiced in the presence of God in which we become more than ourselves while remaining ourselves.

EUGENE H. PETERSON

You, God, are my God, earnestly I seek you;
I thirst for you, my whole being longs
for you, in a dry and parched land
where there is no water.

PSALM 63:1 NIV

Day 13

Charging
My Spiritual Batteries

I will satisfy the weary soul, and every
languishing soul I will replenish.
JEREMIAH 31:25 ESV

I agonized about the situation I was facing. What can I say? If there was a degree in worry, I'd have graduated at the top of my class…and gone on for a master's degree.

I did extensive research online. I talked to close friends and family—probably way more than they wanted. And as the weeks went by, I became worn down in every way.

And then I heard God's whisper in my soul, "You haven't spent much time talking to Me about it." What if I'd prayed about the circumstances as much as I'd whined and worried about them?

Over the next few days, I poured out my heart to my Father. I soaked in the promises in His Word. And you know what? He recharged the batteries of my soul. The overwhelming weariness seeped away as I rested in Him—the place where I should have gone in the first place.

Sweet friends, have you let life wear down your spiritual batteries? Talk to the One who has all the answers to whatever you're going through.

Father, help me to pray about things
more than I whine about them.
Thank You for giving rest for my soul. Amen.

Stop what you are doing long enough to enjoy the sunset, listen to a special song that lifts you up, or pick up the phone and share some special thought with a caring friend.

BARBARA JOHNSON

His divine power has given us everything we need for a godly life through our knowledge of him who called us by his own glory and goodness.

2 PETER 1:3 NIV

By reading the Scriptures, I am so renewed
that all nature seems renewed around me
and with me. The sky seems to be a pure,
a cooler blue, the trees a deeper green.
The whole world is charged
with the glory of God, and I feel fire
and music under my feet.

THOMAS MERTON

Day 14

·····~❧❧❀❦❦~·····

Find Rest for Your Soul

This is what the LORD says: "Stand at the crossroads and look; ask for the ancient paths, ask where the good way is, and walk in it, and you will find rest for your souls."

JEREMIAH 6:16 NIV

Soul rest—that's what we are seeking. We don't want physical rest, though we could use a bit more of that too. No, we need rest for our inner beings, for our hearts and minds, for the core of our existence. We need that deep, satisfying rest that truly restores and enables us to face the new day.

Jeremiah gives us the road map to find it. If the road you're on is full of frustration and heartache and turmoil, stand at the crossroads. Stop and ask for directions! Check the map—God's Word—for a better route. Ask for ancient paths, where the good way is, and walk that way. Choose the crossroad to rest. This may require a change of direction, and we are not always comfortable with change. But when our destination is rest, we can gladly follow the good way to reach it.

*I have trouble following directions, God, so I need You
to walk beside me on this journey to rest. Amen.*

Oh, the joys of those who do not follow the advice of
the wicked.... But they delight in the law of the LORD,
meditating on it day and night. They are like trees planted
along the riverbank, bearing fruit each season. Their leaves
never wither, and they prosper in all they do.

PSALM 1:1–3 NLT

Thus said the Lord GOD, the Holy One of Israel, "In
returning and rest you shall be saved; in quietness and in
trust shall be your strength."

ISAIAH 30:15 ESV

Sit in the companionship of God—the One who shows up
and can be seen.

DALLAS WILLARD

I know the Bible is inspired because it inspires me.

D. L. MOODY

The law of the LORD is perfect,
reviving the soul;
the testimony of the LORD is sure,
making wise the simple.

PSALM 19:7 ESV

Day 15

···◦◦◦✦◦◦◦···

Sensing His Presence

The LORD replied, "I will personally go with you…
and I will give you rest—everything will be fine for you."
EXODUS 33:14 NLT

I lay down with my granddaughter for a nap but eased myself up when I was sure she was asleep. She awoke shortly afterward. To my comment on her short nap, she replied: "I got up because I couldn't feel you anywhere." I'm reminded of a quote from A. A. Milne: "Piglet sidled up to Pooh from behind. 'Pooh!' he whispered. 'Yes, Piglet?' 'Nothing,' said Piglet, taking Pooh's paw. 'I just wanted to be sure of you.'"

God's presence in our lives is a lot like that. We sense and feel it, and it does indeed afford us rest and reassurance. In David's words in Psalm 16:11, "You make known to me the path of life; you will fill me with joy in your presence, with eternal pleasures at your right hand" (NIV).

In Psalm 27:4, the psalmist proclaims, "One thing I ask from the LORD, this only do I seek: that I may dwell in the house of the LORD all the days of my life, to gaze on the beauty of the LORD and to seek him in his temple" (NIV). David didn't fully grasp the implications of his wish, but we'll share its fulfillment with him.

Restore and rejuvenate me
with Your presence, Lord. Amen.

When You said, "Seek My face," my heart said to You, "Your face, LORD, I will seek."

PSALM 27:8 NKJV

In happy moments, praise God. In difficult moments, seek God. In quiet moments, worship God. In painful moments, trust God. Every moment, thank God.

RICK WARREN

The Christian life is to live all of your life in the presence of God.

R. C. SPROUL

In the presence of God, joy is inevitable.

KENDRA GRAHAM

Jesus, the very thought of Thee
With sweetness fills my breast;
But sweeter far Thy face to see,
And in Thy presence rest.

BERNARD OF CLAIRVAUX

Here Today, Gone Tomorrow

People are like grass; their beauty is like a flower in the field. The grass withers and the flower fades.

1 PETER 1:24 NLT

It's tough to hear, but oh, so true. This life is short.

This may sound grim at first, but viewing life as short offers us great hope.

Something happens when we see our lives as blessedly temporary. We have the energy to endure. We rejoice for what we have, not covet what we don't have. Everything good and lovely that passes through our hands becomes a privilege. When we understand that life is short, we see the trials of life from a proper perspective.

When we take the long view of parenting, marriage, and daily struggles, we sense every frustration. We crave comfort and the pleasures of this world—not the pleasure that comes from abiding in Christ.

When we base our hope in this earthly life, we'll struggle

to drum up joy. But when we anchor our hope in the next life, we receive joy that transcends our daily struggles. We know that, someday, Jesus will wipe away every tear. He will restore and heal us.

This view, and only this view, makes the wait worth it.

Jesus, teach me to number my days, weighing everything in light of eternal significance. Amen.

Joy is the infallible sign of the presence of God.

PIERRE TEILHARD DE CHARDIN

Our light affliction, which is but for a moment, is working for us a far more exceeding and eternal weight of glory, while we do not look at the things which are seen, but at the things which are not seen. For the things which are seen are temporary, but the things which are not seen are eternal.

2 CORINTHIANS 4:17–18 NKJV

Teach us to number our days that we may get a heart of wisdom.

PSALM 90:12 ESV

Abide in me, and I in you.

As the branch cannot bear fruit by itself,

unless it abides in the vine,

neither can you, unless you abide in me.

I am the vine; you are the branches.

Whoever abides in me and I in him,

he it is that bears much fruit, for apart

from me you can do nothing.

JOHN 15:4–5 ESV

Day 17

·····⊶∘≫✦≪∘⊷·····

Trusting Him in Our
Wounded Places

"I will restore you to health and heal your wounds,"
declares the LORD.

JEREMIAH 30:17 NIV

We all have wounds. The kind on the inside. Some are surface wounds. Some go deep. It's tempting to focus on them and allow our wounds to define us. But in Christ we are not defined by our wounds; we're defined by Jesus. He is the One who came to heal the brokenhearted and set the captive free. No wound was beneath His attention when He walked this earth, and no brokenness was beyond His ability to mend.

The same Jesus who healed the blind man, pardoned a woman caught in adultery, and allowed a bleeding woman to touch His garment is moving on our behalf.

We can trust Jesus with our wounded places. We can trust He will be gentle and wise as He heals. He will not move more quickly than we can. He will not begin

51

a surgery before we are strong enough for it. His steady goal is to restore us to health, and He will see our healing through to the end.

Jesus never gives up on us. He is always working within us. We can rest in His love. We can trust His skill. It's okay to surrender to His healing touch.

*Thank You, Lord, for healing my wounds
and restoring me to health. Amen.*

God will actually reframe our history and memories to us as He heals us.

STASI ELDREDGE

Christ is the Good Physician. There is no disease He cannot heal; no sin He cannot remove; no trouble He cannot help. He is the Balm of Gilead, the Great Physician who has never yet failed to heal all the spiritual maladies of every soul that has come unto Him in faith and prayer.

JAMES H. AUGHEY

I will make rivers flow on barren heights,
and springs within the valleys. I will turn
the desert into pools of water,
and the parched ground into springs.
I will put in the desert the cedar
and the acacia, the myrtle and the olive...
so that people may see and know,
may consider and understand,
that the hand of the LORD has done this.

ISAIAH 41:18–20 NIV

Day 18

···❦❦❦···

Taking Time

He makes me lie down in green pastures, he leads me
beside quiet waters, he refreshes my soul.
PSALM 23:2–3 NIV

"I'm going outside," I told the caregiver as I hurried out
the door. My mother had been confined to the bed for several months, and it hurt my heart to see her so helpless.
Once a stout woman with the energy of the bunny battery,
now she required assistance with even the simplest of tasks.
Between watching her decline, moving to North Carolina,
and starting a whole new career, I had just about had it
with life. I had to get out of that house for a moment.

Leaving lifelong friends in Florida didn't help. I didn't
have local friends or even time for them. Plus, I lived
in the country, and although beautiful, it added to my iso-
lation. Sure, I attended farmers markets and sold products
in town. That didn't matter—depression enveloped me,
making it hard to breathe.

On that particular day, I sobbed all the way to our pas-
ture and lay down in the grass. "I need You, Lord." I stared

up at the clear sky. Wind rustled through green leaves. The smell of pine filled the air. I rested. Breathed. Took time to just *be*. And became grateful.

I'd been working too hard. My soul was starved for spiritual food—time alone with God. Depression knocked me on my back to rest in green pastures. And He restored my soul. He knew just what I needed.

---

*Lord, thank You for seeing me, for never taking
Your eyes from me, for making me lie down so You
can restore my soul. Thank You for reminding me
that You care for me even while I am caring for others.
You are my strength. I rest in You. Amen.*

God is looking for people who will come in simple dependence upon His grace and rest in simple faith upon His greatness. At this very moment, He's looking at you.

JACK HAYFORD

God walks with us. He scoops us up in His arms or simply sits with us in silent strength until we cannot avoid the awesome recognition that yes, even now, He is here.

GLORIA GAITHER

Come to me, all you who are weary
and burdened, and I will give you rest.
Take my yoke upon you and learn from me,
for I am gentle and humble in heart,
and you will find rest for your souls.
For my yoke is easy and my burden is light.

MATTHEW 11:28–30 NIV

Day 19

The Rest of Repentance

This is what the Sovereign LORD,
the Holy One of Israel, says: "In repentance and rest
is your salvation, in quietness and trust is your strength."

ISAIAH 30:15 NIV

My stomach churned as I waited to explain what had happened at school. For a normally good student, getting in trouble felt like the end of the world. I wanted to hide, but I knew my teacher would be waiting for my mother's call. Coming clean was the only way to find peace.

Just as I couldn't find peace until I'd confessed what had happened at school, we don't find true rest and peace until we confess our sins and repent before the Father. Repentance brings rest. Repentance means we can stop trying to justify ourselves. We can stop wasting energy on worry and fear. We can rest in God's promise of forgiveness and restoration. His forgiveness is complete; we don't have to add anything to what Christ has already done. Instead of anxiety, we can breathe in grace and peace. Instead of cramming more events into our calendars and piling more on our plates, we can give ourselves permission to enjoy moments of peace and stillness in God's presence. We can discover the quiet strength of trusting God to do what He has said He will do.

---

*Lord, thank You that repentance
leads me to rest. Amen.*

Therefore, if anyone is in Christ, he is a new creation. The old has passed away; behold, the new has come.

2 CORINTHIANS 5:17 ESV

Whoever conceals their sins does not prosper, but the one who confesses and renounces them finds mercy.

PROVERBS 28:13 NIV

Instead of concentrating on your problems and getting discouraged, focus on God and meditate on His promises for you. You may have fallen down, but you don't have to stay down. God is ready, willing, and able to pick you up.

JOYCE MEYER

I, even I, am he who blots out
your transgressions, for my own sake,
and remembers your sins no more.

ISAIAH 43:25 NIV

Day 20

Press Pause

Those who hope in the LORD will renew their strength.
They will soar on wings like eagles; they will run
and not grow weary, they will walk and not be faint.

Isaiah 40:31 NIV

I raced home from work on a beautiful October day, hoping to squeeze in one last bike ride before the weather turned. I hurriedly changed into my riding kit and hit the road, pedaling like mad to finish my route before dark.

But I hadn't eaten since lunch, nor had I had much water. Still miles from home, my stomach felt queasy, my knees went weak, and I all but lost my balance. I bonked, as they say.

Fortunately, I'd tucked an energy bar into my jersey. A brief stop, a quick bite, a long draw from the water bottle, and I was back in business.

It's possible to bonk spiritually too. Take life too hard, too fast, with too little attention to your inner life, and you may find yourself emotionally empty, unable to go on. Sadly, even the good things in life can be exhausting.

Stop. Give yourself a time out. Feed on the Word. Allow the fresh breeze of His Spirit to wash over you. This will renew your strength.

Lord, give me some spiritual calories today and renew my strength. Amen.

Open my eyes, that I may behold wonderful things from Your law…. Your word is a lamp to my feet and a light to my path. The unfolding of Your words gives light.

PSALM 119:18, 105, 130 NASB

As the rain and the snow come down from heaven and do not return there without watering the earth and making it bear and sprout and furnishing seed to the sower and bread to the eater; so will My word be which goes forth from My mouth; it will not return to Me empty, without accomplishing what I desire, and without succeeding in the matter for which I sent it.

ISAIAH 55:10–11 NASB

Refresh my heart, Lord,
Renew my love.

REBECCA ST. JAMES

Day 21

Let Jesus Move Your Mountain

"Not by might nor by power, but by my Spirit,"
says the LORD of hosts.

ZECHARIAH 4:6 NKJV

Close your eyes and look at your mountain—that very large thing that's keeping you from moving forward. Is it fear or anger? Maybe a health issue or personal dilemma? Whatever it is, it's big! And after doing everything in your power to change it, sweet talk it, beat it senseless, or ignore it, you end up exhausted and suddenly aware that it's simply too mammoth for you to move.

Girl, don't you know that anything God has put your name on will never require force? He is the Lord of the meek; the Prince of Peace; the One who said, "Be still, and know I am God!" In our fiercest efforts to move things around, we take the responsibility away from the One who allowed them there in the first place. What God requires from us is to hand over everything to Him...*everything*.

It's grace that we don't have to fight for what belongs to us. Jesus will handle it, so just sit back and let your Man do the heavy lifting!

My dear God, in all my crazy effort,
I somehow forgot that You are in control.
Remind me that I don't have to be strong
when it's Jesus moving the mountains. Amen.

Don't tell God how big your mountain is. Tell your mountain how big your God is.

ANONYMOUS

He said to me, "My grace is sufficient for you, for My strength is made perfect in weakness." Therefore most gladly I will rather boast in my infirmities, that the power of Christ may rest upon me.

2 CORINTHIANS 12:9 NKJV

The LORD is my strength and my shield; in him my heart trusts, and I am helped; my heart exults, and with my song I give thanks to him.

PSALM 28:7 ESV

Do not fear, for I am with you;
do not anxiously look about you,
for I am your God. I will strengthen you,
surely I will help you, surely I will uphold you
with My righteous right hand.

Isaiah 41:10 nasb

Day 22

My Quiet Place

Jesus often withdrew to lonely places and prayed.
LUKE 5:16 NIV

When my son and I moved, we left our home, church, friends, and everything familiar. I underestimated the impact of giving up my home office, which had been my work area for freelancing and my place to meet with God. We'd moved in with my parents, so privacy was almost impossible to find. I longed for a special spot for prayer, reflection, or to pray over the phone with a friend without anyone overhearing.

I found the perfect haven while taking a walk—a bench that was just secluded enough to feel like a secret getaway. That became my place to escape to when I needed a moment alone with God to cry out to or thank Him, to rest my mind after a stressful day, or to connect with a prayer partner. Every walk that includes a stop at the bench—even for only a moment—calms me in a unique way.

Jesus needed "lonely places" to meet with His heavenly

Father, and so do we. They can be hard to find, but once found, they become sacred. Where is your quiet place? When is the last time you spent a few precious minutes there?

Lord, provide the private moments
that I need with You today. Amen.

David was greatly distressed…. But David found strength in the LORD his God.

1 SAMUEL 30:6 NIV

Snuggle in God's arms. When you are hurting, when you feel lonely or left out, let Him cradle you, comfort you, reassure you of His all-sufficient power and love.

KAY ARTHUR

The soul is never less alone than when it is alone with God.

SAMUEL CHADWICK

One of the best gifts we can give ourselves is time alone with God.

JOYCE MEYER

We need silence to be alone with God,
to speak to Him, to listen to Him,
to ponder His words deep in our hearts.
We need to be alone with God in silence
to be renewed and transformed.
Silence gives us a new outlook on life.
In it we are filled with the energy of God
Himself that makes us do all things with joy.

MOTHER TERESA

Day 23

⸱⸱⸱⸱⸱⸱⸱⸱⸱⸱⸱⸱⸱⸱⸱⸱

Grace in the Face of Failure

Out of his fullness we have all received grace
in place of grace already given.

JOHN 1:16 NIV

Perfectionism is a joy-stealer, especially when it's a lifestyle. But we don't have to be perfectionists to feel like we've failed. Feelings of failure can blindside us. Our failures can be as simple as forgetting to return a call or set an alarm or as frustrating as burning dinner. And they can be as complicated as struggling in relationship with someone important to us.

God never thinks of us as failures. When He looks at us, He sees the success of Jesus. That doesn't mean we never mess up; it means His grace is right there waiting for us when we do. Not only has God already given us that wonderful, covering grace that fills us with Christ's righteousness, but He also offers empowering grace so we can forgive ourselves and move forward. When we need to respond to our place of struggle and rectify the situation, He gives more grace! Through His Spirit, He guides us, showing us how to handle difficult circumstances, and then He carries us through the experience by His grace.

It's *all* Him! Hallelujah! Pause. Breathe in the grace. It's always there, given freely.

Embrace it.

Father, when I'm tempted to berate myself,
please help me pause, accept the grace already mine,
and move forward. Amen.

The Lord passed before him and proclaimed, "The Lord, the Lord, [is] a God merciful and gracious, slow to anger, and abounding in steadfast love and faithfulness."

EXODUS 34:6 ESV

Your worst days are never so bad that you are beyond the reach of God's grace. And your best days are never so good that you are beyond the need of God's grace.

JERRY BRIDGES

Grace is the voice that calls us to change and then gives us the power to pull it off.

MAX LUCADO

Let us come boldly to the throne
of our gracious God. There we will receive
his mercy, and we will find grace
to help us when we need it most.

HEBREWS 4:16 NLT

Day 24

Have I Been Here Before?

He brought me forth also into a large place;
he delivered me, because he delighted in me.

PSALM 18:19 KJV

Sometimes the only way to move forward is to look back.

The cares of work and family and money and health seem too heavy. Tension tightens the cords in your neck and presses against your temples. You wonder how you can shoulder any more.

Stop and ask: *Have I been here before? Have I experienced this in the past?* Yes. I've carried these burdens before. I've felt this anxiety. *What happened the last time?* I called out to God, and He heard my cry. He gave me His peace. He brought me through it. He will again. Because He delights in me.

It takes discipline and practice to stop and look back, to remember God's faithfulness, to focus on the fact that He delights in you. Take a few minutes every day this week to write out some verses that bring to mind God's peace and presence—verses like Matthew 11:28: "Come to me, all you who labor and are heavy-laden, and I will give you rest" (NKJV). Carry them with you for those times when you need to be reminded.

Lord, in those times when my cares
seem too heavy, help me to turn to You
and recall Your faithfulness. Amen.

Cast all your anxiety on him because he cares for you.

1 PETER 5:7 NIV

Be still, my soul; thy God doth undertake
To guide the future as He has the past.

KATHARINA VON SCHLEGEL

You, O Lord, are a God of compassion and mercy, slow to get angry and filled with unfailing love and faithfulness.

PSALM 86:15 NLT

Cast your burden on the LORD, and he will sustain you; he will never permit the righteous to be moved.

PSALM 55:22 ESV

In all His relations with His people,
God is faithful. He may be safely
relied upon. No one ever yet really trusted
Him in vain. We find this precious truth
expressed almost everywhere
in the Scriptures, for His people need
to know that faithfulness is an essential
part of the divine character.
This is the basis of our confidence in Him.

A. W. PINK

Day 25

·····→∋∂✕ᏻᏻᏻᏻᏻᏻᏻᏻ←·····

God's Safe House

The LORD is a shelter for the oppressed,
a refuge in times of trouble.

PSALM 9:9 NLT

Where was your safe place when you were a child? I had a treehouse with walls and a sturdy ladder—high up above everyone else. There I could escape the noise, conflict, or the crowd. I could dream. I felt comfortable, cozy, and somehow protected.

Perhaps you had a bedroom corner, a homemade tent, or a spot in the backyard. But where do you go today, now that you're a grown-up and it seems impossible to hide from the world?

Even if you have a favorite easy chair, reality encroaches as cell phones beckon and people demand that you meet their immediate needs.

But who will meet *your* need for security and safety?

Where can you still the pounding of your heart, breathe calmly, and know deep in your soul that you are truly loved and accepted?

Only in the Lord. As the psalmist says, He alone is our shelter when we are oppressed. God alone is our "refuge in times of trouble."

He is the best safe house ever! No matter where we are or what is happening, we can rest in His protective presence.

---

*Lord, the world is scary; help me turn
to You for continual refuge. Amen.*

He will cover you with his feathers, and under his wings you will find refuge; his faithfulness will be your shield and rampart.

PSALM 91:4 NIV

God of peace, you are at the center of my life, a strong refuge of peace in the whirlwind of my pain. I look to you for strength and a constant assurance of hope.

JOYCE RUPP

You are a hiding place for me; you preserve me from trouble; you surround me with shouts of deliverance.

PSALM 32:7 ESV

Trust in Him at all times, you people;
pour out your heart before Him;
God is a refuge for us.

Psalm 62:8 nkjv

Day 26

Seclusion Sentinels

At daybreak, Jesus went out to a solitary place.
LUKE 4:42 NIV

"By myself" has gotten a bad rap in our garrulous society. Instead of taking time alone to think about a situation, we often engage our mouths in stream-of-consciousness gushing or compulsively "self-express" via texting. But are our minds and hearts as nimble as our fingers? Do we take time to acquaint ourselves with the self we're expressing—or the God we want to express?

Unfortunately, it never occurs to many of us to regard solitude as an indulgence—if we see its benefits at all. Yet without it, we're diminished. Jesus needed and craved time alone with His Father, but the Gospels make clear that He no more demanded privacy than He claimed the prerogatives of His deity.

Does the call to Christlikeness demand the same of us? I don't believe it does. Loving others as we do ourselves requires that we place their needs on par with our own—not that we deny ours altogether. That's why they're called needs.

Poet Rainer Maria Rilke applied this concept to marriage, observing that "a good marriage is that in which each appoints the other guardian of his solitude." Whose solitude do you guard, and who returns the favor for you? Your effectiveness depends on it.

Teach me, Lord, to appreciate and prioritize solitude,
both in my life and in others'. Amen.

When you pray, go away by yourself, shut the door behind you, and pray to your Father in private. Then your Father, who sees everything, will reward you.

MATTHEW 6:6 NLT

Solitude is the furnace of transformation. Without solitude, we remain victims of our society and continue to be entangled in the illusions of the false self.

HENRI NOUWEN

True silence is the rest of the mind, and is to the spirit what sleep is to the body, nourishment and refreshment.

WILLIAM PENN

When He had sent the multitudes away,
He went up on the mountain
by Himself to pray.
Now when evening came,
He was alone there.

MATTHEW 14:23 NKJV

Day 27

⤞⤞⤞❈❈❈⤝⤝⤝

For the Overwhelmed,
Worried, and Discouraged

*You, O LORD, are a shield around me; you are my glory,
the one who holds my head high.*

PSALM 3:3 NLT

When we feel overwhelmed, when it seems life is on the offensive and we're assailed by the fiery darts of the enemy, the Lord is our shield. He surrounds us with His presence. There are no chinks in this protection. He will not allow anything to harm us that is not meant for our ultimate good. We need not fear any attack.

When we feel worried about what others think, when we feel our reputation is under scrutiny or our good name has been wrongly maligned, the Lord is our glory. We don't need to strive to make everyone happy. We have nothing to prove. His glory is complete and sufficient; we need only to trust and obey.

When we feel discouraged or downtrodden, as if we're carrying the weight of the world on our shoulders, the Lord is the lifter of our head. He reaches out to us, gently invites us to lift our eyes up from our difficult circumstances and look full in His wonderful face. We need not let our circumstances have the final say, but instead meet His loving gaze and be filled with peace.

Tender Father, make me sensitive to Your presence.
Fill me with confidence in Your protection, and replace
my anxiety with Your perfect peace. Amen.

Be anxious for nothing, but in everything by prayer and supplication with thanksgiving let your requests be made known to God. And the peace of God, which surpasses all comprehension, will guard your hearts and your minds in Christ Jesus.

PHILIPPIANS 4:6–7 NASB

Many things about tomorrow I don't seem to understand but I know Who holds tomorrow and I know He holds my hand.

IRA STANPHILL

Turn your eyes upon Jesus,
Look full in His wonderful face;
And the things of earth
Will grow strangely dim
In the light of His glory and grace.

HELEN H. LEMMEL

Day 28

···∞∂∂❊❧ᴄᴄᴄ···

Perfect Peace

You will keep him in perfect peace,
whose mind is stayed on You.

Isaiah 26:3 nkjv

The worst is when you can't sleep. The turmoil and troubles you've dealt with during the day rob you of rest at night. They fight it out while you try to shut them out; they replay themselves with "if only" and "how dare they" commentaries attached.

But God's Word offers a better rest, a sweeter peace. He promises that we can quiet our restless spirits with His Spirit of rest. He offers "peace that passes understanding" and "peace, not as the world gives." His peace is perfect.

So what do we do to find that perfect peace? Keep our minds on Him. We must focus on God's power, not the tumultuous circumstances. We fix our hearts on Him so that He can fix what concerns us. We stay our thoughts on our faithful Father, who does all things well. This is not an easy task! The noisy problems still call to us; the worries stir up a racket in the background. But when we center our minds on the One in control, He gives perfect peace.

———————————

Dear Lord, I cannot turn away from the worrisome distractions of my life without Your help. Please direct my focus to You and provide for me Your perfect peace. Amen.

———————————

In peace I will lie down and sleep, for you alone, O LORD, will keep me safe.

PSALM 4:8 NLT

May the Lord of peace Himself continually grant you peace in every circumstance.

2 THESSALONIANS 3:16 NASB

If you refuse to be hurried and pressed, if you stay your soul on God, nothing can keep you from that clearness of spirit which is life and peace. In that stillness, you know what His will is.

AMY CARMICHAEL

Peace does not dwell in outward things,
but within the soul; we may preserve it
in the midst of the bitterest pain
if our will remains firm and submissive.
Peace in this life springs from
acquiescence to, not in an exemption
from, suffering.

FRANÇOIS FÉNELON

Day 29

Lord, You Are...

LORD, you are my God;
I will exalt you and praise your name.

ISAIAH 25:1 NIV

"Dear God—" Ever get stuck there, or on the sigh that follows? In the midst of busyness and daily stress, it's sometimes hard to form the words.

Think of what you know to be true of God and tell Him. "Lord, You are..." You are love. You are peace. You are holy and pure and patient and true. Lord, You are my strength, my shield, my hope, my hiding place, my strong fortress.

Reflect on the names of God. *El Shaddai*: All sufficient, Almighty. *Jehovah Jireh*: The Lord will provide. *Adonai*: My great Lord.

Maybe these reminders will prime the pump and prayer words will flow. Maybe the first one that comes to mind is where you need to stay for now. "Lord, You are my peace," or "Jesus, I love You." And isn't that enough? Enough to connect you with the heart of God, to bring you to that abiding place? There will be days when your praise will gush like water from an underground spring, and then there will be the times when you simply need to quietly abide. On those days, it is enough to say, "Lord, You *are.*"

Father, remind me, moment by moment,
who You are. Amen.

O LORD, our LORD, how majestic is your name in all the earth!

PSALM 8:9 ESV

Let all who take refuge in You be glad, let them ever sing for joy; and may You shelter them, that those who love Your name may exult in You.

PSALM 5:11 NASB

Where does your security lie? Is God your refuge, your hiding place, your stronghold, your shepherd, your counselor, your friend, your redeemer, your savior, your guide? If He is, you don't need to search any further for security.

ELISABETH ELLIOT

I will proclaim the name of the LORD.
Oh, praise the greatness of our God!

DEUTERONOMY 32:3 NIV

Day 30

Unplug

Your ears will hear a word behind you,
"This is the way, walk in it,"
whenever you turn to the right or to the left.

ISAIAH 30:21 NASB

There is no such thing as silence in our world. We wake to the sound of an alarm. Notifications ring on our phones before breakfast. We drive in a bubble of podcasts or streaming music. Phone calls, television, commercials, car horns—sound invades our souls from dawn till dusk.

And that's fine. Except that the voice of God is still and small and easily drowned out by other sounds.

We didn't invent this predicament. Jesus faced it too, even without a smartphone. To escape from the clamor of voices that enveloped Him through every waking moment, Jesus unplugged. He got away from people, from community, from noise, to be alone with the Father.

Why do we find that so hard to do? Is it because we feel obligated to be in touch with those around us? Are we duty-bound to be constantly wired? Is it even possible to unplug?

It is, and you can. You have permission to turn off the noise. You are allowed to go for a walk without your phone. You are not required to reply to every text message. You don't need anyone's approval to be alone with God. You have His invitation, and that's enough.

Lord, I want to hear Your voice above all others.
Speak to me, I pray. Amen.

God has spoken very boldly about His desire to be a presence in our lives. If I want to heal the ache and loneliness in my own life, one of the things I need to do is get away, alone with God…. In the silence, God will speak to you most powerfully. Too often His words to us get muffled, lost, or covered by the crowd of many noises both inside and outside of us. We must have a quiet heart in order to hear God's distinctive message to us.

TIM HANSEL

I will instruct you and teach you
in the way you should go; I will counsel you
with my loving eye on you.

Psalm 32:8 niv

Day 31

····⤙⤙❦❦⤚⤚····

Pausing to Receive His Delight

Your love delights me, my treasure, my bride.
Your love is better than wine,
your perfume more fragrant than spices.

SONG OF SOLOMON 4:10 NLT

Did you know you make Jesus happy? That you actually *delight* Him?

Pause a moment and remember a wedding ceremony where it was obvious the groom adored his bride. Think about the look in his eyes as she came down the aisle. Did his smile stretch wide? Maybe he wiped a tear. He gazed at her like there was no one else in the room, and she couldn't take her eyes off him either.

That's how Jesus looks at *you*, His treasured bride. When He chose the cross, He did it for the joy set before Him. See, the Father promised the Bridegroom a wife.

And oh, how *delighted* He is with His Father's choice! *You!*

When you love Jesus, He likes it better than sipping the finest wine. When you snuggle up close to Him for intimate companionship, He enjoys your fragrance. He pauses to simply breathe you in.

Just like you do Him.

It's a ring of delight. He loves you, and you feel loved. You love Him, and He feels loved. Delight enfolds you both. Unending. Circling back and forth between you.

O Jesus, what joy to dwell in our circle of delight! Amen.

The LORD your God is living among you. He is a mighty savior. He will take delight in you with gladness. With his love, he will calm all your fears. He will rejoice over you with joyful songs.

ZEPHANIAH 3:17 NLT

God loves each one of us as if there were only one of us to love.

ST. AUGUSTINE

If God had a refrigerator, your picture
would be on it. If He had a wallet,
your photo would be in it.
He sends you flowers every spring
and a sunrise every morning....
Face it, friend. He is crazy about you!

Max Lucado

Day 32

Royal Rest

May the LORD answer you when you are in trouble;
may the God of Jacob make you secure!

Psalm 20:1 NET

King David's status didn't match the statistic on insomnia. As a young, fugitive warrior fleeing from his father-in-law, he was neither a widow nor over sixty-five. Even though he fell outside the research stats, he still had trouble succumbing to sleep.

Few have experienced danger like David. As he hid from enemies, he had many opportunities to remain awake and camp in dangerous circumstances. Predatory animals roamed dusty, hot deserts. Seasoned soldiers trailed behind with intent to kill. Lack of supplies and water threatened his safety during the day as well as at night.

Because he had been stretched to develop battle skills that supplemented God's call to Israel's throne, he also learned of the Lord's faithfulness, provision, and comfort. Each morning brought new challenges, but he survived the night through dependence on the One who never failed.

David's trials kept him awake many nights, yet he continued to depend on God. The Lord who protected David from the lion and bear also stands guard during our darkest nights. Situations that steal peace can help develop our wavering trust into the confidence of a king in a cave.

Lord, I look to You for safety and rest
in my cavern of distress. Amen.

A God wise enough to create me and the world I live in is wise enough to watch out for me.

PHILIP YANCEY

Though I walk in the midst of trouble, You will revive me; You will stretch forth Your hand against the wrath of my enemies, and Your right hand will save me.

PSALM 138:7 NASB

Did you never run for shelter in a storm, and find fruit which you expected not? Did you never go to God for safeguard, driven by outward storms, and there find unexpected fruit?

JOHN OWEN

If the Lord be with us, we have no cause
of fear. His eye is upon us,
His arm over us, His ear open
to our prayer, His grace sufficient,
His promise unchangeable.

JOHN NEWTON

Day 33

Stop Taking Yourself
So Seriously

*I am the only one left, and now
they are trying to kill me, too.*

1 KINGS 19:14 NLT

Ever been so exhausted that you felt like you can't go on?

In 1 Kings 19, we see Elijah totally spent. Not long after the prophet's mountaintop experience, where he called down fire on the prophets of Baal, we glimpse Elijah undone, sitting under a tree, praying for death.

Sometimes life's valleys can pop out of nowhere and leave us echoing Elijah's prayer, "I have had enough, LORD" (vs. 4). Next, the prophet takes a much-needed nap, and God sends an angel with food and water. It's amazing what a little rest and nutrition will do.

One thing topped Elijah's list of worries. He believed God's work would end if he died. Elijah thought everything depended on him.

Ever felt like the world rested on your shoulders? For

Elijah, God set the record straight. "I will preserve seven thousand in Israel who have never bowed down to Baal" (vs. 18). God had a plan that Elijah knew nothing about.

Like Elijah, we often take ourselves too seriously, thinking our families and jobs rely solely on us. This kind of thinking wrings us dry, but trusting God gives life.

---

*Jesus, help me not take myself too seriously,
and when I do, teach me to laugh at myself. Amen.*

Laughter is the most beautiful and beneficial therapy God ever granted humanity.

CHARLES R. SWINDOLL

Trust in the LORD with all your heart, and lean not on your own understanding; in all your ways acknowledge Him, and He shall direct your paths.

PROVERBS 3:5–6 NKJV

Hope fills the afflicted soul with such inward joy and consolation that it can laugh while tears are in the eye, sigh, and sing all in a breath; it is called "the rejoicing of hope."

WILLIAM GURNALL

Whatever it is probably won't go away,
so we might as well live and laugh
through it. When we double over laughing,
we're bending so we won't break.
If you think your particular troubles
are too heavy and too traumatic to laugh
about, remember that laughing is like
changing a baby's diaper. It doesn't solve
any problems permanently, but it makes
things more acceptable for a while.

BARBARA JOHNSON

Day 34

High upon a Rock

In the day of trouble he will keep me safe in his dwelling;
he will hide me in the shelter of his sacred tent
and set me high upon a rock.

Psalm 27:5 niv

The rocks rose like ramparts through massive trees. I loved to escape here and climb to their heights. One summer afternoon, I scaled the rocky bluffs to my favorite vantage point. The previous night's storm had left the rocks slippery, and I made my way carefully. Just as I peaked, I noticed out of the corner of my eye a gray flutter. There, nestled in a tiny cleft in the rock, was a baby bird, all alone. There was no soft nest beneath him, but the space was a perfect shelter from storm and predator.

How often I recall that tiny bird, hidden away in its shelter from the storm, high upon the rock! Our God promises that when the storms of life come, He will keep us safe in His dwelling, He will hide us in His shelter, high upon a rock. Are you in need of shelter today? Close your eyes and imagine you are that little bird, safely tucked away from harm. You are secure in God's hiding place.

Lord, when the storms of life are threatening,
be my shelter and my safe place. Amen.

Keep me as the apple of your eye; hide me in the shadow of your wings.

PSALM 17:8 ESV

When we stand in the middle of a lifestorm, it seems as if the storm has become our way of life. We cannot see a way out. We are unable to chart a course back to smoother waters. We feel defeated—and broken…. Will we yield up that brokenness to the resources of One who calms the winds and the waves, heals the brokenhearted, and forgives the most grievous of sins?

VERDELL DAVIS

You are my hiding place and my shield; I hope in Your word.

PSALM 119:114 NKJV

Sometimes the Lord rides out the storm
with us and other times He calms
the restless sea around us.
Most of all, He calms the storm
inside us in our deepest inner soul.

LLOYD JOHN OGILVIE

Day 35

••••••◦•◦•◦••◦••••••

My Soul Needs a Rest

Learn from Me…and you will find rest for your souls.
MATTHEW 11:29 NKJV

As the beach umbrella flapped gently in the wind, I soaked in the sounds around me. Seagulls squawking as they glided overhead. The crash of the waves as they broke onto the shore. My grandchildren laughing as they played in the water. The whisper of the ocean breezes as they wafted by.

Warm sunshine shone down on me, relaxing muscles that had been tight with tension when I arrived that day. You see, when our family vacation finally began, I was weary. Physically. Emotionally. And, yes, even spiritually.

Long months of illness had taken their toll. My sixteenth surgical procedure had arrived unexpectedly in the form of emergency eye surgery that left me on bed rest for several weeks. I'd used up all my emotional reserves. It felt like there was nothing left.

But as I sat on the sand that day with my family, I felt a sweet peace seep into my soul. I rested, soaking in the beauty of His creation, looking at the majesty and grandeur of the ocean, and was reminded once again of the majesty and grandeur of a God who can bring rest to our souls.

———————

Father, thank You for sending moments
that bring sweet rest to my soul. Amen.

———————

It is wisdom to take occasional furlough. In the long run, we shall do more by sometimes doing less. On, on, on forever, without recreation, may suit spirits emancipated from this "heavy clay," but while we are in this tabernacle, we must every now and then cry halt, and serve the Lord by holy inaction and consecrated leisure.

Charles Spurgeon

We all know we need rest from work, but we don't realize we have to work hard just to rest. We have to plan for breaks. We have to schedule time to be unscheduled. That's the way life is for most of us. Scattered, frantic, boundaryless busyness comes naturally. The rhythms of work and rest require planning.

Kevin DeYoung

You gave abundant showers, O God;
you refreshed your weary inheritance.

PSALM 68:9 NIV

Day 36

·····❦·····

The Best Place to Hide

Rescue me from my enemies,
LORD, for I hide myself in you.

PSALM 143:9 NIV

No one liked to play hide and seek with little Noah. He was the best hider even in the least creative hiding spaces. Every game with him ended with all the children giving up, finally calling out to him to just come on out, declaring him the winner. One day he hid so well that his playmates concluded he had left the game. They went on to another activity. Two hours later, Noah's mother found him sleeping under her kitchen sink.

There is a hiding place for the children of God that is so safe, so hidden, that the enemy cannot find it. The one who hides there can rest in her position, knowing she is secure. Enemies withdraw, retreat from the battle. Pressures abate, and the weary soul finds rest. This best of hiding places is in the Lord Himself.

We all wish to hide from the battle some days. Even in

the busiest of times, when trials press in on every side, we can withdraw to a safe and secure hiding place. That place is the Lord. As we hide ourselves in Him, He will give us rest from the battle and deliver us from our enemies.

Lord, I hide myself in You today. Amen.

You are my hiding place;
You fill my broken heart with songs.

SARA GROVES

You shall hide them in the secret place of Your presence from the plots of man; You shall keep them secretly in a pavilion from the strife of tongues.

PSALM 31:20 NKJV

You are my hiding place;
you will protect me from trouble
and surround me
with songs of deliverance.

PSALM 32:7 NIV

Day 37

······᠉᠊ᡃᢓᢞ᠊᠊᠊᠊ᢞᡩᡃ᠊᠊······

The Full Breath
of Restoration

For God was in Christ, restoring the world to himself,
no longer counting men's sins against them
but blotting them out.

2 Corinthians 5:19 TLB

Sometimes we breathe in Christ's work on the cross in tiny, stifled breaths. We thank Him for forgiving this sin, that fault, this situation. God wants us to take a full, deep, restorative breath. One that covers all of life—every past, present, or future mistake. When Christ returned us to God's favor, God completely blotted out *every* sin.

The Bible calls us new creations. It says our sinful selves have *died*. At the core, we are no longer rotten with sin; we are righteous in Jesus! In our centermost person is light, joy, beauty, and glory. There is *Jesus*.

When God looks at us, He sees the righteousness—the right living, the goodness—of His Son. Isn't that amazing?

Sure, we may have some bad habits—old thinking and

behaviors—that God is changing, but that is not *who* we are any longer. We are the righteousness of God in Christ, and He promises to complete the good work He started in us. He reveals Himself to us, and as we get to know Him better, we are transformed into the image of His precious Son.

Dear God, thank You for establishing me in righteousness and making me like Jesus. Amen.

If anyone is in Christ, he is a new creature; the old things passed away; behold, new things have come.

2 CORINTHIANS 5:17 NASB

Conversion does not make us perfect, but it does catapult us into a total experience of discipleship that affects—and infects—every sphere of our living.

RICHARD J. FOSTER

God made him who had no sin to be sin for us, so that in him we might become the righteousness of God.

2 CORINTHIANS 5:21 NIV

I am about to do something new.
See, I have already begun!
Do you not see it? I will make
a pathway through the wilderness.
I will create rivers in the dry wasteland.

ISAIAH 43:19 NLT

Day 38

·····❧❧❁❧❧······

Enjoying Restful Seasons

My beloved spoke and said to me, "Arise, my darling,
my beautiful one, come with me. See! The winter is past;
the rains are over and gone. Flowers appear
on the earth; the season of singing has come."

Song of Solomon 2:10–12 niv

What delight to enjoy the restful seasons God plans for us!
Times when His love is so tangible we can almost hear Him
whisper, "Come away with Me, dear one. Smell the clean
fragrance that comes after the rain. Pick the flowers. Find
pictures in the clouds.

"Come away, My friend! Splash in the river. Put your
toes in the warm sand. Just rest. Enjoy. Experience the
blessing I've prepared for you.

"Come away, My beloved! Play. Laugh! Notice the
ladybug upon the leaf, the tiny bluets in the grass, the
hummingbird at its feeder. Enjoy reflection. Quiet.

"Gather at the campfire, the fireplace. Sit on your deck
or at the coffee shop. Tell stories. Sing songs. Delight in

friends and family. Turn up the football game and pass out the chips and salsa!

"Enjoy solitude. Light a candle and play Mozart. Read a good book.

"Enter fully into the gifts I give You. Enjoy the restful times I've prepared."

Jesus, please help me to enjoy the restful seasons You give me, whether they last a minute or a year. Amen.

So I commend the enjoyment of life, because there is nothing better for a person under the sun than to eat and drink and be glad. Then joy will accompany them in their toil all the days of the life God has given them under the sun.

ECCLESIASTES 8:15 NIV

It is the sweet, simple things of life which are the real ones after all.

LAURA INGALLS WILDER

God...richly supplies us with all things to enjoy.

1 TIMOTHY 6:17 NASB

There is nothing dreary and doubtful
about [life]. It is meant to be
continually joyful…. We are called
to a settled happiness in the Lord,
whose joy is our strength.

AMY CARMICHAEL

Day 39

Pick Some Flowers

Consider how the wild flowers grow.
They do not labor or spin. Yet I tell you, not even
Solomon in all his splendor was dressed like one of these.

LUKE 12:27 NIV

"Go outside and play!" I heard those words a thousand times as a child, and I uttered them a thousand more as a parent. Getting the kids out of doors is a cure for boredom and an antidote for crankiness. There's something about fresh air and exercise that opens the mind and frees the soul.

Perhaps the best result of being outdoors is that it reminds us how great God is and how wonderfully present He is with us. If we have eyes to see it, even the tiniest flower can be a symbol of the fact that God has created, ordered, and continues to sustain a marvelously complex universe.

Go outside and allow the wonder drug of fresh air to invade your lungs. Walk along whatever green space is available to you. And be on the lookout for God's most delicate and beautiful works of art, His flowers. With each bloom you see, remember that God cares for you even more than these.

---

*Lord, thank You, thank You, thank You
for the way You provide for me. Amen.*

Consider the ravens, for they neither sow nor reap; they have no storeroom nor barn, and yet God feeds them; how much more valuable you are than the birds!

LUKE 12:24 NASB

Climb the mountains and get their good tidings. Nature's peace will flow into you as sunshine flows into trees. The winds will blow their own freshness into you and the storms their energy, while cares will drop off like autumn leaves.

JOHN MUIR

Reading about nature is fine, but if a person walks in the woods and listens carefully, he can learn more than what is in books, for they speak with the voice of God.

GEORGE WASHINGTON CARVER

Fair are the meadows,

fairer still the woodlands,

Robed in the blooming garb of spring;

Jesus is fairer, Jesus is purer,

Who makes the woeful heart to sing.

MÜNSTER GESANGBUCH

Day 40

Sail-through Window

Jesus said to them, "Come and have breakfast."

JOHN 21:12 NASB

Early each morning, the drive-through windows are packed in my town. But one long-ago morning on the beach, the God of the universe fired up a skillet.

In gentle waters, the despondent disciples cast out nets under sunny, clear skies. Their beloved Teacher was gone and the night of work had not brought in fish.

They may have laughed with cynical grins at the suggestion of the strange fellow on the beach and thrust out the net more in frustration than in faith. When the heavy load could not be hauled in, John recognized the stranger as the Lord-who-provides.

Jesus cooked up a remedy for the heavy hearts of His disciples as He stirred the embers. He not only offered His presence but met a basic need for a work-weary crew of fishermen.

I've felt like the disciples. When separated from the Lord in my despair, I've neglected my basic physical needs.

Although the disciples sailed into breakfast, I take a break to cook up a meal and anticipate His blessing of provision. Spending time in my own kitchen allows me an opportunity to reflect and enjoy God's presence, something I'll forfeit if I drive on through.

Lord, stir the embers of my heart
as I begin my day with You. Amen.

If you have a special need today, focus your full attention on the goodness and greatness of your Father rather than on the size of your need. Your need is tiny compared to His ability to meet it.

BILL PATTERSON

A firm faith in the universal providence of God is the solution of all earthly troubles.

B. B. WARFIELD

Man shall not live by bread alone, but by every word that proceeds from the mouth of God.

MATTHEW 4:4 NKJV

Our Father in heaven,
Hallowed be Your name.
Your kingdom come.
Your will be done
On earth as it is in heaven.
Give us this day our daily bread.
And forgive us our debts,
as we forgive our debtors.
And do not lead us into temptation,
but deliver us from the evil one.
For Yours is the kingdom and the power
and the glory forever. Amen.

MATTHEW 6:9–13 NKJV

Day 41

A Troubled Heart

Let not your heart be troubled;
you believe in God, believe also in Me.

JOHN 14:1 NKJV

There is something about a walk on the beach that will clear your mind and quiet your heart. When I lived in Florida, I often took long walks on the beach. Meandering beyond the crowd, I'd plop down on the wet sand and stare at the ocean.

Waves crashed against sandy shores. Seagulls glided through clear skies. Occasionally, a dolphin stuck his fin through swirling waters. His bottle-like nose and glassy eye seemed to smile as he splashed the air.

Breathtaking.

As I sat, I'd sing. Praise would erupt from my soul and disappear behind me into the strong wind. No one heard me. I could barely hear. But God did.

After singing, I would pray. Pouring out my requests to the Lord, I felt my heart lighten. Knowing that I have a Father who hears me in a strong wind on a sandy beach always calmed my troubled heart.

After an hour or so, I would walk home, sloshing feet through a foamy shore while gazing at coquina shells pushing up for a breath.

Maybe you have a troubled heart today. Let me give you a prescription—get alone with God. Seek His face. Praise and pray.

And, it's free.

Lord, thank You for calming my troubled heart. Amen.

An unpeaceful mind cannot operate normally. Hence the apostle teaches us to "have no anxiety about anything" (Philippians 4:6). Deliver all anxious thoughts to God as soon as they arise. Let the peace of God maintain your heart and mind.

WATCHMAN NEE

Why, my soul, are you downcast? Why so disturbed within me? Put your hope in God, for I will yet praise him, my Savior and my God.

PSALM 43:5 NIV

See, God has come to save me.

I will trust in him and not be afraid.

The LORD GOD is my strength and my song;

he has given me victory.

ISAIAH 12:2 NLT

Day 42

·········⊱⊰·········

The Burden of Stuff

But godliness with contentment is great gain, for we brought nothing into the world, and we cannot take anything out of the world. But if we have food and clothing, with these we will be content.

1 TIMOTHY 6:6–8 ESV

Having beloved possessions can bring us a lot of pleasure, but it can also be a burden. A parent dies, leaving behind a houseful of memory-laden items that need to go… somewhere. A child returns from college, stashing an apartment load of boxes in the basement at the very moment her parents want to downsize.

Attaching cherished memories to material items is normal; it's a part of being human, but it makes giving them up difficult. At the same time, the more we cluster stuff around us, the more it weighs us down, perhaps even making us feel claustrophobic and anxious. We're surrounded by memories we want to keep, but we can't even breathe.

Yet none of this is eternal. We will one day leave it all behind. And if we're honest, it's usually the memory we cherish, not the item we associate it with. If we take Paul's words to heart, we can step away from material goods and find a new place of contentment and peace, one box at a time.

Lord, please help me keep my eyes and mind on You. Remind me that only You are eternal in my life. Amen.

Keep only those things that speak to your heart. Then take the plunge and discard all the rest. By doing this, you can reset your life and embark on a new lifestyle.

MARIE KONDO

Trust in the LORD and do good; dwell in the land and cultivate faithfulness. Delight yourself in the LORD; and He will give you the desires of your heart.

PSALM 37:3–4 NASB

I have held many things in my hands, and have lost them all; but whatever I have placed in God's hands, that I still possess.

MARTIN LUTHER

I have learned in whatever state I am,
to be content: I know how to be abased,
and I know how to abound.
Everywhere and in all things I have learned
both to be full and to be hungry,
both to abound and to suffer need.
I can do all things through Christ
who strengthens me.

PHILIPPIANS 4:11–13 NKJV

Day 43

·····➷➷➫✳︎❧❧❦···

Experiencing Peace
in the Midst of Anxiety

My flesh and my heart fail, but God is the strength
of my heart and my portion forever.

Psalm 73:26 nkjv

You might believe that you can't experience anxiety and peace at the same time, but that's just not true. If you are someone who suffers from chronic anxiety, those feelings might not be going away any time soon. But you can still experience the peace of Christ in your heart even as you fight the lies of anxiety in your head.

This is because God is the strength of our heart. When we rely on His power rather than our own, we can experience a peace that surpasses understanding. Rather than allowing the anxious feelings to overwhelm us, we can trust in God. And yes, there will be times when we will fail because we are still living in the flesh, but that's okay. When we fail, God is there to pick us back up and be our strength.

Even while battling the anxiety we feel within, we can trust in a God who is above all and is pouring out His peace on us.

Heavenly Father, I am so grateful for the strength and peace I receive from You even when I fail or succumb to anxiety. Remind me daily of Your great love for me. Amen.

When a man has no strength, if he leans on God, he becomes powerful.

D. L. Moody

On the day I called, you answered me; my strength of soul you increased.

Psalm 138:3 esv

He'll carry us when we can't carry on.

Jerry Salley and Steven Curtis Chapman

As you trust Me more and more, you are able to receive Me and My blessings abundantly. Be still, and know that I am God.

Sarah Young

I am convinced that nothing can ever
separate us from God's love.
Neither death nor life, neither angels
nor demons, neither our fears for today
nor our worries about tomorrow....
No power in the sky above or in the earth
below—indeed, nothing in all creation
will ever be able to separate us from
the love of God that is revealed
in Christ Jesus our Lord.

Romans 8:38–39 NLT

Day 44

······❧❧❧❦❦❦❦······

Resting in His Arms

Yes, my soul, find rest in God; my hope comes from him.
PSALM 62:5 NIV

"Night, night, Addie," I addressed my four-year-old grand-daughter. "Settle down now."

"I am cuddled down."

I like that turn of phrase. Makes me think of hunker-ing down in preparation for an extended rest. I vicariously sense an exhalation of stress, initiating a mental and physi-cal letting go.

When Adelyn shares my bed, I invariably feel during the night her little hand reaching over to contact my arm and her exploring toes to stroke my leg. Her breathing deepens with those confirming touches. Addie finds repose in my nearness.

"Security," observes an unknown author, "is not the absence of danger but the presence of God, no matter what the danger." My hope comes from God precisely because I rest in Him. I'm awed by Jesus's prayer from the garden: "Just as you are in me and I am in you," He addresses His

Father on behalf of all believers, "may they also be in us" (John 17:21 NIV). But the "in" in Psalm 62:5 functions differently—it's about having confidence in someone else. But the image that comes unbidden to my mind is of being enveloped by the same God who also dwells in me.

Father God, help me tonight to cuddle down,
encircled in the inviolable security of Your embrace. Amen.

The LORD is good to those who wait for Him, to the soul who seeks Him. It is good that one should hope and wait quietly for the salvation of the LORD.

LAMENTATIONS 3:25–26 NKJV

In place of our exhaustion and spiritual fatigue, God will give us rest. All He asks is that we come to Him…that we spend a while thinking about Him, meditating on Him, talking to Him, listening in silence, occupying ourselves with Him—totally and thoroughly lost in the hiding place of His presence.

CHARLES R. SWINDOLL

The LORD is my rock, my fortress
and my deliverer; my God is my rock,
in whom I take refuge, my shield
and the horn of my salvation, my stronghold.

PSALM 18:2 NIV

Day 45

Breathe in the Middle of the Chaos

The eternal God is your refuge, and underneath are the everlasting arms.

DEUTERONOMY 33:27 NIV

Life is busy and fast paced, whether it's because you're a mom keeping up with energetic children or you have a job that requires you to be always on the move. You may be wondering when life will slow down so you can rest, but sometimes slowing down isn't an option, and the chaos can be overwhelming. Life doesn't always slow down when we need it to.

When we can't stop the commotion, we need to take a moment to stop and take a breath in the middle of the chaos. We need to close our eyes and remember who is holding us. God has not left us, and the disarray we are experiencing is no surprise to Him. His arms are everlasting, and in them we find security. We don't have to fear that the chaos will consume us, because He is protecting us.

Do not fear, because He has overcome the world—and that includes the chaos surrounding you.

Dear Father, even when I feel like I am drowning, You are always holding me. Thank You for Your loving arms that protect me from the chaos of life. Amen.

We went through fire and through water; yet you have brought us out to a place of abundance.

PSALM 66:12 ESV

I've found that when I take my eyes off my needs and focus on how awesome and powerful God is, my troubles disappear in His presence.

BEN CERULLO

If you look at the world, you'll be distressed. If you look within, you'll be depressed. But if you look at Christ, you'll be at rest.

CORRIE TEN BOOM

I have told you all this so that you
may have peace in me. Here on earth
you will have many trials and sorrows.
But take heart, because I have
overcome the world.

JOHN 16:33 NLT

Day 46

Lifting the Weight of Anxiety

Anxiety weighs down the heart,
but a kind word cheers it up.

<small>PROVERBS 12:25 NIV</small>

When I was a child, we made blanket forts. We would carefully place the chairs so the blankets would not fall and cover us. Then we would gather our things and place them in the fort. We could play for hours under those blankets, until the natural force of gravity caused them to fall on top of us. We would, of course, then scream and wiggle our way out from under the blankets and rebuild our fort again.

Anxiety is much like the blanket fort, except when the blanket falls, it can be heavy and no matter how much we wiggle, we cannot escape without help. If we have not kept proper things in the fort with us, our escape can be long and difficult. We cannot lift the weight of the blanket alone.

If we keep the Word of God in our hearts, we will always have the proper things to lift the weight of the anxiety blanket we are under. God's Word—His constant good Word—when applied by our personal faith, gives us a strength much stronger than the weights of this world. The weight of anxiety has no chance against the mighty Word of God.

Father God, fill my heart and mind with Your Word.
Plant it deeply in my soul so I always have
Your strength to come to when the weight
of this world becomes too much. In Jesus's name, Amen.

Now what is food for the inner man? Not prayer, but the Word of God; and here again, not the simple reading of the Word of God, so that it only passes through our minds, just as water passes through a pipe, but considering what we read, pondering it over and applying it to our hearts.

GEORGE MÜLLER

The word of the LORD is tried; He is a shield to all who take refuge in Him.

PSALM 18:30 NASB

All Scripture is given by inspiration of God,
and is profitable for doctrine, for reproof,
for correction, for instruction in
righteousness, that the man of God
may be complete, thoroughly equipped
for every good work.

2 TIMOTHY 3:16–17 NKJV

Day 47

·····➤➣✹✺✹❧ᙣᙘᙗ·····

Rest and *Laziness* Aren't Synonyms

Then He replied, "My presence will go with you,
and I will give you rest."

Exodus 33:14 hcsb

My earliest memories were of being surrounded by women who never stopped moving and serving. If my grandmother sat down, she had something in her hands—crochet, knitting, even green beans to snap. My mother never just sat; she had her watercolors and sketchbook out.

Staying busy was all I knew. Even now, I always have a project with me to keep my hands busy.

While that seems like a laudable characteristic, there can be a dangerous flaw there if we're not careful. Somewhere along the way, I'd developed the opinion that *rest* and *laziness* were synonyms. That attitude began to shape the way I judged myself. I only felt I had worth when I'd accomplished something and when I was busy.

That's not the way God sees us. He loves us as we are

and wants to spend time with us. He's not checking our to-do list and handing out gold stars. God designed us for rest.

It wasn't until I untied my to-do list from my sense of worth, that I could experience God's rest to the fullest.

---

*Dear Lord, help me remember that You
designed me for rest. Amen.*

The world clamors, "Do more! Be all that you can be!" But our Father whispers, "Be still and know that I am God."

JOANNA WEAVER

The Lord said to her, "My dear Martha, you are worried and upset over all these details! There is only one thing worth being concerned about. Mary has discovered it, and it will not be taken away from her."

LUKE 10:41–42 NLT

Christ's protest is not against work, but against anxious thought.

HENRY DRUMMOND

The best antidote for anxiety is frequent
meditation upon God's goodness, power,
and sufficiency.... Nothing is too big,
and nothing is too little to spread
before and cast upon the Lord.

A. W. PINK

Day 48

Soul Care

I will be glad and rejoice in your unfailing love,
for you have seen my troubles, and you
care about the anguish of my soul.

PSALM 31:7 NLT

How much did you spend last year keeping your body
and your physical health in shape? When we add up the
resources devoted to eating right, exercising regularly, and
maintaining medically, we discover taking care of ourselves
is a big investment. And rightly so.

But how much time and resources did you spend last
year on keeping your *soul* healthy?

Because it's harder to pinpoint the state of our inner
life, we often neglect soul care, saying that we will get
around to it…eventually. Until one day we finally call out
to God concerning "the anguish of my soul."

Today we can change. We can carve out time to spend
doing those things that nourish our faith and our sense of
God's "unfailing love."

Why not set a time and place to pray, to praise Him,

and then share your concerns and needs? Use a devotional that helps you invest in God's Word every single day. Meditate on those words as true *soul food*.

Sound impossible? We make time for what is most important. God sees our troubles and wants to help us.

Just begin.

---

*Lord, help me make time with You
a joy and priority. Amen.*

In the morning, LORD, you hear my voice; in the morning I lay my requests before you and wait expectantly.

PSALM 5:3 NIV

Time alone with [God] can be one of the greatest time savers of your life. It is in your time alone with the Lord that you can surrender the burden and the anxiety of the load to Him. You can also find the perspective to be delivered from the truly nonessential things that often seem important.

BILL THRASHER

———————————

As we walk through each day, responding
to the needs of those around us,
we can become physically,
emotionally, and spiritually depleted.
God has a never-ending supply of grace,
strength, and wisdom available that
He wants to flow through us to others.
And we need to keep coming back into
His presence to get our supply replenished.

NANCY LEIGH DeMOSS

———————————

Day 49

The Overwhelming Life

From the ends of the earth, I cry to you for help
when my heart is overwhelmed. Lead me to the towering
rock of safety, for you are my safe refuge.

PSALM 61:2–3 NLT

Feeling crushed by responsibilities and duties is common to most of us. The pressures of work, family, church, and other commitments weigh down on us, threating to overwhelm us. When we look at all we have to take care of, a sense of panic sets in, making us desire nothing more than a long nap and a chair on a beach. Yet finding time to breathe, to find a few moments of peace, feels impossible. There's just too much to do!

These are the times that turning to God for help is more important than ever. In Him who is our refuge, we can find a clear path. He will provide the peace, hope, and guidance we need to get through each task one by one and to maintain our sense of calm direction.

By focusing on Him, we gain perspective. As we remember what's important to Him, we can prioritize with more clarity…and we may even learn to say no more often, whenever someone starts a sentence, "Can you—?"

———————————————

Lord, help me turn to You when I am overwhelmed.
Grant me a sense of peace, an open heart,
and a clear vision to deal with all that I've been handed.
You are my only refuge. Amen.

———————————————

If you need wisdom, ask our generous God, and he will give it to you. He will not rebuke you for asking.

JAMES 1:5 NLT

Whenever you say yes to something, there is less of you for something else. Make sure your yes is worth the less.

LYSA TERKEURST

Should we feel at times disheartened and discouraged, a simple movement of heart toward God will renew our powers. Whatever He may demand of us, He will give us at the moment the strength and courage that we need.

FRANÇOIS FÉNELON

When you pass through the waters,
I will be with you;
and when you pass through the rivers,
they will not sweep over you.
When you walk through the fire,
you will not be burned;
the flames will not set you ablaze.

Isaiah 43:2 niv

Day 50

Seasons of Life

[She] is like a tree planted by streams of water,
which yields its fruit in season.

PSALM 1:3 NIV

Often when my heart seems to be withering, Psalm 1 comes to mind. I envision a comforting, peaceful scene—a lush, fruitful tree, firmly established beside a stream—and I long for that!

The stability of the scene seems undeniable—a tree firmly rooted, unaffected by the whims of society, the fickleness of friends, and ever-changing circumstances. But then I notice verse 3: "in season." Looking out at the stark white of winter, I'm reminded that not every season is fruitful and productive. That's how my spirit feels right now—cold, barren, unproductive, even dead at times.

Yet, I take comfort in my roots. As I examine the depths of my soul, I find a green, living core, nourished by the water of the Word. The Source is always there—providing life-giving moisture to my roots.

The hope of spring assures me that I will not die as I

endure this season. I can hang on through the stark barrenness of winter—which has a beauty all its own—knowing that God will not forget me. Spring rains are coming!

God, help me to delight in Your Word,
nourishing my roots in You, that I might
flourish in the next season. Amen.

If we are to bear much fruit…then the best model for spiritual maturity is seasons. Fruit grows in seasons, and all seasons are necessary for growing it. And seasons are as much about what is not happening as what is. It has as much to do with inactivity as with activity, waiting as with working, barrenness as with abundance, dormancy as with vitality.

Mark Buchanan

I pray that from his glorious, unlimited resources he will empower you with inner strength through his Spirit. Then Christ will make his home in your hearts as you trust in him. Your roots will grow down into God's love and keep you strong.

Ephesians 3:16–17 nlt

As you therefore have received
Christ Jesus the Lord, so walk in Him,
rooted and built up in Him and established
in the faith, as you have been taught,
abounding in it with thanksgiving.

COLOSSIANS 2:6–7 NKJV

Day 51

Take Time to Celebrate

Go, eat your food with gladness,
and drink your wine with a joyful heart,
for God has already approved what you do.
ECCLESIASTES 9:7 NIV

"I guess that's enough for now," I said, wiping my forehead. "I'll finish up in a minute." I'd been doing yard work all day but still had a few sticks to pick up.

"Are you kidding?" Heather asked. "It's after eight o'clock."

"But it stays light so long now. And there's so much to be done."

"It can wait," she said firmly. "There's only one Saturday this week, and you've missed most of it. Time to unwind."

Relaxation doesn't come naturally to achievement-oriented people like me—and perhaps you? Something in the back of the mind constantly prods us on. *You could be doing more. You haven't earned a rest. Now that the kids are asleep, you should be getting some work done.*

Recognize that voice for what it is: your inner demon,

trying to convince you both that you must earn the love of others and that you never will.

God has accepted you. You don't need to earn His approval. In fact, you can't. So relax. Celebrate the good you've done today, and let tomorrow worry about itself.

Lord, teach me to feel the blessing of Your approval and to dance in Your delight. Amen.

For the happy heart, life is a continual feast.

PROVERBS 15:15 NLT

In almost everything that touches our everyday life on earth, God is pleased when we're pleased. He wills that we be as free as birds to soar and sing our Maker's praise without anxiety.

A. W. TOZER

Make a joyful noise to the LORD, all the earth!… Come into his presence with singing!… For the LORD is good; his steadfast love endures forever, and his faithfulness to all generations.

PSALM 100:1–2, 5 ESV

We can be satisfied. We are loved,
wanted, seen, delighted in, provided for,
cherished, chosen, known,
and planned on. We are set apart,
believed in, invited, valued,
of immeasurable worth, and blessed.

STASI ELDREDGE

Day 52

Delighting

Take delight in the LORD,
and he will give you the desires of your heart.

PSALM 37:4 NIV

Walking to school, five-year-old Adelyn catches things I miss. We encounter spider webs of differing intricacies, including one this morning with its impressive mustard-and-black artist at work. Others shimmer with dewdrops. Dandelions tantalize along the route, the fist-clutched bouquet growing for the handoff to Granna. Berries and acorns drop Addie to a crouch. And when she isn't still and absorbed, she's skipping, twirling, and calling to my attention other "cool moves."

In the verse above, the psalmist invites us to focus our delight on the Lord, following up with an incredible promise. I can do no better than to make sure the desires of my heart in turn delight the Lord.

We too easily miss the reality that our doting Father finds delight in delighting us. "Having given us the package," reflects Oswald C. Hoffman, "do you think God will deny us the ribbon?" I particularly love the rendering of Zephaniah 3:17 in the older (1984) NIV: "The LORD…will take great delight in you, he will quiet you with his love, he will rejoice over you with singing."

Help me to take delight in You, Father,
even as You delight in me. Amen.

When my anxious thoughts multiply within me, Your consolations delight my soul.

PSALM 94:19 NASB

I will be fully satisfied as with the richest of foods; with singing lips my mouth will praise you. On my bed I remember you; I think of you through the watches of the night.

PSALM 63:5–6 NIV

May my meditation be pleasing to him, for I rejoice in the Lord.

PSALM 104:34 ESV

God cannot give us a happiness
and peace apart from Himself,
because it is not there.
There is no such thing.

C. S. Lewis

Day 53

Trusting in the Name of God

Those who know your name trust in you, for you, LORD,
have never forsaken those who seek you.

PSALM 9:10 NIV

There are times in every believer's life when he or she feels like God is very far away. Those times may come when he or she has sinned, suffered a tremendous setback in life, lost a loved one, or let quiet time with God slip by the wayside.

Have you ever felt that way? You know you should probably read your Bible or go to church, but you just don't feel like it. All you can do is sit.

What is the one thing that remains constant during those times? What is the only thing you can cling to? The name of the Lord. Often all you can do is whisper His name. Say it over and over. You know the power that is there, but you are not able to get beyond the mere utterance of that name.

But with each breath that you speak His name, you bring yourself closer to reconnecting with Him and feeling the power that is within you because you are His.

Do you need refreshment today? Just sit quietly and breathe the name of Jesus.

Lord, thank You that grasping hold of Your power
in my life is as simple as speaking Your name. Amen.

Lord, there is no one like you! For you are great, and your name is full of power.

JEREMIAH 10:6 NLT

I have a great need for Christ; I have a great Christ for my need.

CHARLES SPURGEON

The name of the Lord is a fortified tower; the righteous run to it and are safe.

PROVERBS 18:10 NIV

May the Lord answer you in the day of trouble; may the name of the God of Jacob defend you.

PSALM 20:1 NKJV

In biblical times, a name represented
a person's character. God's name
represents His attributes, His nature.
His name is a statement of who He is.
And He has many names!
Each reveals something of His power
and love and purposes toward you.

KAY ARTHUR

Day 54

The Balm of Palms

I am the LORD your God, who upholds your right hand,
who says to you, "Do not fear; I will help you."

ISAIAH 41:13 NASB

Confidence and independence are admired characteristics. Yet it's common to long for helping hands when faced with challenging tasks or situations.

Even Biblical heroes experienced fear and became weary. Moses must have felt relieved to have assistance from his brother to help with the release of an entire enslaved nation. Jeremiah had the strength to move forward after the Lord explained that the plans He had for him were not to harm him. And Isaiah, struggling to be faithful and deliver an unpopular message, kept on going after God offered His presence as incentive.

Busy, productive hands can become weary and tired after a long haul of challenging tasks and situations. The delight to be offered assistance during times of great struggle may not change the outcome of a trial. Yet the comfort experienced when a burden is shared within adversity may free up reserves of strength thought already spent and bring great relief.

The Lord offered help by extending His hand to ancient travelers on their paths of faith. We can glean hope and vitality from their examples by taking hold of the same hands that are outstretched still.

Father God, instead of wringing my hands,
I extend them toward You. Amen.

It is not the cares of today but the cares of tomorrow that weigh a man down. For the needs of today, we have corresponding strength given. For the morrow, we are told to trust. It is not ours yet. It is when tomorrow's burden is added to the burden of today that the weight is more than a man can bear.

GEORGE MacDONALD

Strengthen the weak hands, and make firm the feeble knees. Say to those who are fearful-hearted, "Be strong, do not fear! Behold, your God will…come and save you."

ISAIAH 35:3–4 NKJV

If you pour yourself out for the hungry
and satisfy the desire of the afflicted,
then shall your light rise in the darkness
and your gloom be as the noonday.
And the LORD will guide you continually
and satisfy your desire in scorched places
and make your bones strong; and you shall
be like a watered garden, like a spring
of water, whose waters do not fail.

ISAIAH 58:10–11 ESV

Day 55

❧❧❀❦❦

Barefoot Blessing

Do not come near here; remove your sandals
from your feet, for the place on which you
are standing is holy ground.

<small>EXODUS 3:5 NASB</small>

If I were a biophysicist, I could both explain and understand the concept of grounding, a process to replenish electrons. Something good is supposed to happen to our nervous system when our bare feet contact dirt, grass, or sand.

Moses didn't remove his sandals to upload some atoms but to obey God's command from a burning bush. God didn't reveal Himself in the palatial surroundings of Moses's youth but in a dry, barren land where a much older, humble Moses stood barefoot and fearful, after years of exile amid the desert sheep.

When I need to reassess my path, I could look for inspiration within the hygienic halls of modern success. But I remember Moses. The iconic leader of Israel spent most of his career with dusty feet. As a seasoned shepherd, he'd trained for the long journey through the wilderness to a promised land.

I don't want to miss a chance to hear from the Lord wherever He calls. Maybe it is the electrons, but the blessing of digging my toes into the earth draws me closer to the One who made the sands.

Lord, humble me down to my toes
as I seek to hear from You. Amen.

God, interrupt whatever we are doing so that we can join You in what You're doing.

FRANCIS CHAN

I am persuaded that love and humility are the highest attainments in the school of Christ and the brightest evidences that He is indeed our Master.

JOHN NEWTON

He has shown you, O mortal, what is good. And what does the LORD require of you? To act justly and to love mercy and to walk humbly with your God.

MICAH 6:8 NIV

166

The high and lofty one who lives in eternity, the Holy One, says this: "I live in the high and holy place with those whose spirits are contrite and humble. I restore the crushed spirit of the humble and revive the courage of those with repentant hearts."

Isaiah 57:15 nlt

Day 56

Dwelling Place

If you remain in me and my words remain in you,
you may ask anything you want, and it will be granted!
JOHN 15:7 NLT

Some people relish gardening, digging their hands in the earth, patiently awaiting a harvest. But for the rest of us, Jesus offers some fantastic news.

In John 15, the Son of God likens a relationship with Him to a grapevine. The best part? The Father is the Gardener, not us! God's in charge of all the sweaty work involved with gardening. He does the planting, the pruning, and the weeding.

Jesus lists one job for us to do—produce fruit. It's the vine that determines the type of fruit that grows. The vine supplies the needed nutrients and water. The branch merely holds the fruit.

In this not-so-subtle way, Jesus reminds us that He's in charge here, not us. We blossom and produce fruit by receiving what He supplies, by dwelling in Him and in His Word.

Our natural bent is to grow toward independence, to grow wild and self-sufficient. As you take a moment to breathe, remember where you dwell. Your home is in Christ. Your life is connected to His life, and apart from Him, you can do nothing.

Jesus, teach me how to remain in You—
Your grace, strength, and presence, bearing spiritual fruit
from a position of rest, not work. Amen.

We are responsible to clothe ourselves with Christlike character, but we are dependent on God's Spirit to produce within us His fruit.

JERRY BRIDGES

We have not ceased to pray for you and to ask that you may be filled with the knowledge of His will in all spiritual wisdom and understanding, so that you will walk in a manner worthy of the Lord, to please Him in all respects, bearing fruit in every good work and increasing in the knowledge of God.

COLOSSIANS 1:9–10 NASB

_____

The fruit of the Spirit is love, joy, peace,
longsuffering, kindness, goodness,
faithfulness, gentleness, self-control.
Against such there is no law.

GALATIANS 5:22–23 NKJV

_____

Day 57

··········᠈᠊᠈᠊᠈᠋᠊᠊᠊᠊᠊᠊᠊᠊··········

Praising in Times of Stress

When I am afraid, I put my trust in you. In God,
whose word I praise—in God I trust and am not afraid.
What can mere mortals do to me?

PSALM 56:3–4 NIV

Life is messy. It is all too easy to let it cause us to feel
stressed, in a hurry, and uptight. It's not easy to let go of
busyness and anxiety when the world around us is hectic—
but it can be done.

All of us have a fear of the unknown. An unexpected
medical diagnosis, job loss, death. It can sometimes feel
overwhelming to handle it on our own. Thankfully, we
don't have to. When we feel unable to climb out of the
valley, all we have to do is look up. God has the strength to
silence the voices of fear and anxiety. It is possible to learn
to make faith, not fear, the default reaction.

Faith sees a way, whereas stress and fear see obstacles.
In today's verse, David feared, but he turned to God. He
chose to rely on God's truths, and we should do the same.

True peace will never be found in others, only in God, whose supernatural peace is gained when we let go and trust in Him.

_____

Lord, I have no reason to fear because
You are beside me. Amen.

_____

A Christian's freedom from anxiety is not due to some guaranteed freedom from trouble, but to the folly of worry and especially to the confidence that God is our Father, that even permitted suffering is within the orbit of His care.

JOHN STOTT

"I know the plans I have for you," says the LORD. "They are plans for good and not for disaster, to give you a future and a hope."

JEREMIAH 29:11 NLT

Worry is blind and cannot discern the future, but Jesus sees the end from the beginning. In every difficulty, He has His way prepared to bring relief.

ELLEN WHITE

May the God of hope fill you
with all joy and peace in believing,
so that by the power of the Holy Spirit
you may abound in hope.

ROMANS 15:13 ESV

Day 58

Listen to Music

When they had sung a hymn,
they went out to the Mount of Olives.

Matthew 26:30 niv

My friend is a music professor and concert pianist who has performed all over the world. I enjoy following her travels on social media, seeing photos of the recitals she's given in places like Vienna, Bangkok, Buenos Aires, and Hong Kong. But when she and her husband adopted two small children, I knew that her aggressive schedule would likely be curtailed.

"Will the world stop hearing this beautiful music?" I wondered.

One evening I opened Facebook to see a video she had posted. This one was not from Carnegie Hall or some grand venue in Europe. It was my friend, in her living room, playing "Dance of the Sugar Plum Fairy" from *The Nutcracker* as a lullaby for her children. Within minutes, the same gifted hands that had charmed audiences all over the world had put two little girls to sleep.

Jesus and His disciples sang together on the eve of their painful ordeal. He knew the soothing power of music. Do you?

Music is not merely entertainment or background noise for our daily lives. It is a window into the soul through which God can pour His love and mercy. Open your window.

Lord, let Your beautiful music
soothe my troubled soul. Amen.

Music is God's gift to man, the only art of heaven given to earth, the only art of earth we take to heaven.

WALTER SAVAGE

Praise Him with the sound of the trumpet; praise Him with the lute and harp! Praise Him with the timbrel and dance; praise Him with stringed instruments and flutes! Praise Him with loud cymbals; praise Him with clashing cymbals! Let everything that has breath praise the LORD.

PSALM 150:3–6 NKJV

Music…will help dissolve your perplexities
and purify your character and sensibilities,
and in time of care and sorrow,
will keep a fountain of joy alive in you.

DIETRICH BONHOEFFER

·····❧᙭❧·····

The Encouragement
of a Friend

*Perfume and incense bring joy to the heart,
and the pleasantness of a friend springs
from their heartfelt advice.*

PROVERBS 27:9 NIV

There's nothing like pausing to enjoy the encouragement of a good friend. You know the kind. She has a gentle, focused gaze and *really* listens—with her heart, not just her head. She waits for you to let it all out and, even then, doesn't rush in with unwanted advice. She pays attention to what you're saying and what you're not saying, even while her spirit is attuned to His.

When she speaks, God's law of kindness is upon her lips. Whether the words are what you expected or not, whether they are easy or hard to receive, you know it is heartfelt advice. You can trust her.

We treasure these friends. Even when life gets crazy, we make time to be together. The friend who walks with us in difficulty is the friend we seek out in times of celebration.

Moments with a trusted friend lift burdens and expand joy. Laughter is fuller when shared with a friend. Tears are less devastating. Funny movies are funnier. Marathons are shorter. Coffee even tastes better when paired with good conversation.

Time set aside to be with a good friend is always time well spent.

Thank You, God, for the gift of good friends. Amen.

A generous person will prosper; whoever refreshes others will be refreshed.

PROVERBS 11:25 NIV

They are rich who have true friends.

THOMAS FULLER

They refreshed my spirit and yours also. Such men deserve recognition.

1 CORINTHIANS 16:18 NIV

I cannot even imagine where
I would be today were it not
for that handful of friends who have
given me a heart full of joy.
Let's face it, friends make life a lot more fun.

CHARLES R. SWINDOLL

Day 60

Cabin Comfort

Let us draw near with confidence to the throne of grace,
so that we may receive mercy
and find grace to help in time of need.

HEBREWS 4:16 NASB

Visiting our grandparents' mountain cabin was a summer highlight for my brother Ed and me. We fished with Granddaddy, skipped rocks on the river, and explored trails in wooded areas. A bee sting or skinned knee would occasionally interrupt our play. After Mamie, our grandmother, treated our wounds, we would return joyfully to our outdoor adventures.

Midafternoon, weary from our play, we would head inside to discover a treat Mamie had baked. Her banana nut bread was a favorite, especially when she served it warm with a glass of ice-cold milk.

Whether we required medical care, more fishing worms, or a snack, we could depend on Mamie. She was always there, in the cabin, ready to meet our needs.

Our heavenly Father is ever available to His children.

Not only does He allow us to approach His throne, but He beckons us to bring our praise and petitions. We can completely trust Him to administer grace and mercy regardless of the circumstance. With childlike faith, we can run to Him with every need.

Abba Father, I'm grateful that accepting
Your salvation plan makes Your throne of grace
available to me at any time. Amen.

In him and through faith in him we may approach God with freedom and confidence.

EPHESIANS 3:12 NIV

You did not receive the spirit of bondage again to fear, but you received the Spirit of adoption by whom we cry out, "Abba, Father."

ROMANS 8:15 NKJV

Look at the birds. They don't plant or harvest or store food in barns, for your heavenly Father feeds them. And aren't you far more valuable to him than they are?

MATTHEW 6:26 NLT

Our heavenly Father understands
our disappointment, suffering, pain, fear,
and doubt. He is always there to encourage
our hearts and help us understand
that He's sufficient for all of our needs.

CHARLES STANLEY

Thank You to Our Contributors

Kristel Acevedo

Elizabeth Banks

Michelle Cox

Lauren Craft

Linda Gilden

Jeannette Hanscome

Donn Huisjen

Pauline Hylton

Danetta Kellar

Aleah Marsden

Lucinda Secrest McDowell

Leslie McKee

Becky Melby

Edie Melson

Paula Moldenhauer

Trisha Mugo

Diane Nunley

Leigh Powers

JoHannah Reardon

Jane Reed

Carol Reid

Ramona Richards

Kimberly Shumate

Adria Wilkins

Lawrence Wilson

IF YOU ENJOYED THIS BOOK, WILL YOU CONSIDER SHARING THE MESSAGE WITH OTHERS?

Mention the book in a blog post or through Facebook, Twitter, Pinterest, or upload a picture through Instagram.

Recommend this book to those in your small group, book club, workplace, and classes.

Head over to facebook.com/worthypublishing, "LIKE" the page, and post a comment as to what you enjoyed the most.

Tweet "I recommend reading #RefreshYourSoul by @WorthyPub"

Pick up a copy for someone you know who would be challenged and encouraged by this message.

Write a book review online.

WORTHY®
PUBLISHING

Visit us at worthypublishing.com

 twitter.com/worthypub

 worthypub.tumblr.com

 facebook.com/worthypublishing

 pinterest.com/worthypub

 instagram.com/worthypub

 youtube.com/worthypublishing